Real Estate
Good Life

Real Estate Good Life

HOW I SOLD 250 HOMES LAST YEAR, WORKING NO
EVENINGS, NO WEEKENDS, AND NO FRIDAYS

Bart Vickrey, Real Estate Jedi

ISBN: 1517607760
ISBN 13: 9781517607760

This book is dedicated to the two most important women to ever step foot into my life. My mother, Sandra Shields, and my Bride, Stacey Vickrey. The significance of your contributions to my life is immeasurable. Thank you from the bottom of my heart for everything you've done and continue to do.

Table of Contents

CHAPTER 1

Yetis, Divorce, and Day Drinking

The AirTran 737 touched down at 12:08 p.m. at Cancun International Airport.

Stacey's slumbering head felt like a bowling ball on my shoulder. As the wheels hit the ground, she jostled awake, leaving behind a makeup imprint on my favorite Valparaiso University sweatshirt. I also noticed just a little bit of a slobber trail that she was kind enough to leave behind.

What the hell, I thought to myself. First your heavy drunken head prevents me from reading properly on the plane...and now this!

The girls started drinking early.

We picked up our friends Jeff and Casey Haggerty at their home at five thirty in the morning. The girls rode in the back, and the six-foot-four-inch Yeti rode in the front of my 2008 Jeep Grand Cherokee with me.

I love that Jeep! It's silver with a dark gray leather interior and a built-in Sirius radio for listening to Howard Stern. I've had it since August of 2011, when I bought it for $21,500. It only had 26,000 miles on it. We paid cash. Our car-buying protocol is simple: never buy new and always pay cash.

As soon as I shifted into drive, I heard the familiar sound "sshhhpop" of a champagne bottle. What the hell, I thought, isn't it a little early?

Casey has been known to deliver a complete and unforgiving stress test to her liver on vacation. And Stacey, who only drinks on special occasions, considers vacation a special occasion. So they were off, just like that...let the party start!

We arrived at Midway Airport in Chicago at 6:55 a.m. and had no trouble checking our bags and then getting through security.

We found a spot at the bar at Harry Caray's, as all the seats in the airport restaurant were already filled. Casey ordered a Salty Dog and Stacey a Bloody Mary. Jeff had a water, and I had black coffee.

Now don't get the wrong idea—I enjoy cocktails more than most, but I'm not a good day drinker. Once I start drinking, I don't want to stop, and then I get real tired and am a wreck long before the partying ends.

Several times when I was entertaining with a house full of guests, or especially after a Popcorn Festival, I've had to sneak into my bedroom, lock the door, and pass out! People started calling it the Houdini!

The Popcorn Festival is an annual event in Valparaiso, Indiana, the home of the famous Orville Redenbacher. The city shuts down the main intersection on Lincolnway in front of and around the old courthouse.

There's a parade, several live music stages, and, for me, day drinking. It's one of the only days of the year I permit myself some drinking before dark.

I ordered scrambled eggs, bacon, and wheat toast to go along with my black coffee. Stacey said she wasn't hungry, but when my food arrived it was a different story. "Can I have a bite of your eggs?"

"Sure, honey."

"Oh, that bacon looks good."

Crunch! I'm all for sharing, but this shit happens all the time. Order your own breakfast next time, would ya?

After Harry Caray's we headed toward Concourse A to make our way to the gate. Along the way the girls stopped at Halsted Street Tap. Stacey ordered another Bloody Mary, and Casey a Cape Cod. Jeff caved to the peer pressure and ordered a Captain and Coke.

Now keep in mind that it was barely 8:00 a.m., and there were two dudes sitting in this airport bar completely in the bag. I call it a bar, but it looked more like a well-lit breakfast diner. One of the guys wore a Steelers jersey and had both hands ensconced in black and gold Hulk Hands. And he was casually drinking with this huge rubber hand as if to say, "There's nothing to see here!"

Scorecard: Girls four drinks each, Jeff one, and Bart zero.

I ordered another coffee, and the three of them started in on me... followed by ole Hulk Hands and his red-eye-rimmed counterpart. We all laughed, snapped a few pics, and finally made our way to the gate.

Our flight was at 8:35 a.m., but soon we learned that there would be about a ten-minute delay. The pilot was late coming in on a different flight. No big deal. But it apparently gave Casey time for another gargle of giggle juice, and she promptly sent Jeff back to the bar. Stacey declined his offer for another round as she was only a quarter of the way through her Bloody Mary. And again, the old teetotaler declined.

At this point, my plan was to hold off till late afternoon or early evening, but I wasn't certain these revelers were going to make it that long!

The pilot arrived and we began the boarding process. AirTran has an upgrade they call business class. For an extra $200 per person your bags fly free, and you get to board first. Business class is the first three rows of seats on the plane. And instead of the cramped three seats to a row, it's only two big seats. The girls had upgraded us a couple days before the flight. As soon as we boarded the flight attendants took our drink orders, while the rest of the bums sitting in steerage had to wait until well after liftoff.

"What can I get for you?" I heard from across the aisle. The tall, thin attendant waited on Casey and Jeff's order. She had beautiful dark brown hair and was wearing maybe a touch too much makeup.

"Vodka and club soda." Casey smiled.

"And I'll have a Captain and Coke," said Jeff.

"Uh, Miss, can I go ahead and get two bottles of vodka with that?" Casey quizzed.

Stacey turned to me and asked if I was having a cocktail yet. "No, I'm holding out until we get there."

"Do you care if I have another?"

"Have all you want, but you'll be passed out by noon if you keep it up!"

"I'm only having one more and then waiting until dinner."

Sure, I thought.

About an hour into the three-and-a-half-hour flight Stacey asked, "Can I rest my head on your shoulder?" I reluctantly agreed, but I was really starting to get into the book I was reading, *Start with Why* by Simon Sinek. Stacey was seated to my left, which meant her melon was resting on my left shoulder. I'm left handed, and I was armed with a yellow highlighter as I usually am when reading nonfiction. Dammit!

The sun was shining, and it was a beautiful eighty-four degrees Fahrenheit when we arrived. The resort sent us a van to get from the airport to Playa Mujeres. The ride was about forty-five minutes long.

"Look, there's a donkey in that alleyway!" I said excitedly. There's just something about a donkey that I find marvelous! And don't get me started about a miniature donkey! It's maybe the greatest creature alive. Stacey and I live on forty acres in southeast Valparaiso, Indiana. I tell people all the time that at some point we're getting a miniature donkey for the backyard. I would name him Don Vickrey, middle name Key.

At a stoplight a pink moped pulled up with an attractive yet kind of trashy Mexican lady. She was about twenty-one years old and had on six-inch heels! Standing in front of her—yes, you heard me right—standing in front of her between the seat and the handlebars was a sweet little girl holding a Barbie Doll!

"Viva la Mexico, this is going to be off the chain!" I yelled. Sometimes I say things that I think sound cool, but my daughters always inform me otherwise.

We entered the all-inclusive, adults only, Excellence Playa Mujeres resort after being stopped by two separate security gates. The driver would say our names with a thick accent to the guards who would then flip through the pages on their clipboards. *Vic-r-ray* and *Heggerrrrrrty*.

The van finally arrived outside the grand entrance to the resort. We were immediately welcomed by two mocha-colored bellmen who seemed over the moon to see us. One started heaving our bags out of the back of the van, and the other presented us with a cold washcloth and a chilled glass of champagne! "Now we're talking!" Jeff exclaimed.

I prudishly didn't drink my champagne and quickly realized that the washcloth smelled like lemon-fresh Pledge. I only like lemon in my tea and occasionally in my water. Other than that I'm out!

Stacey rolled her eyes and sipped her bubbly trying to ignore my "rich boy" problems.

We checked in and headed over to our building. Building number seven was in a great location, close to the pools, the main entertainment amphitheater, and the main outdoor bar, which also featured nightly live music.

The room was magnificent! Open, bright, marble, luxurious with an amazing view of the resort, pool and Gulf of Mexico.

Immediately on the right there was a door halfway up the wall. Inside the door was a three-foot by three-foot box. The box was also accessible from the hallway. "What's this for?" I wondered.

"I bet that's for dishes and stuff from room service," Stacey answered.

"Wow, I bet you're right. That's awesome!"

Next to the dumbwaiter was the bathroom—with a marble floor, granite countertops, double sinks, a private commode behind a smoked glass door, and a walk-in shower. The shower alone was the size of my bedroom growing up and had multiple showerheads with one big stainless steel rainfall head in the middle.

The bathroom wasn't completely enclosed. The sunburst-shaped mirrors in front of each sink hung suspended from the ceiling, with block-shaped one-foot-wide walls on either side. Otherwise the room was open. The shower was enormous and had a window overlooking the enormous king-size bed and the spacious living room. You could watch TV while you showered!

The refrigerator stood three and a half feet tall and was completely stocked with full-size Corona beer bottles, Coke and Diet Coke, small bottles of white wine, and small bottles of Corona Light. The fridge was integrated into a beautiful dark mahogany front with a bar area above. Glass shelves hung above the bar. On the shelves were full-size bottles of tequila, rum, whiskey, and red wine.

Along the left-hand wall, next to the fridge and bar area, was a beautiful dresser and then a desk with an office chair. At the end of the room, looking out to the pool and Gulf, were floor to ceiling glass sliders. The enormous glass doors slid open from one end of the room to the other, giving a dramatic open-air tropical feel.

Through the sliders on the left was a huge whirlpool spa and out on the balcony on the left was a queen-size daybed overflowing with fluffy pillows. "Oh my God, this place is incredible!" I yelled.

We met up with the Haggerty's and they gave us a tour of the resort. They'd been the year before and absolutely raved about the place. They didn't oversell it. The resort was incredible, and the atmosphere was immediately calming.

The trip was all inclusive, with no children, nine restaurants, nightly entertainment, continuous live music, and perfect weather—all with my Bride by my side. Looking back, of course, my vision is clearer. Stacey and I were on a cold streak. Our routine had become, well, routine. We were talking less, kissing less, and hugging less. I was in one of my "obsessed with business" modes and felt underappreciated for all of my efforts.

Our time spent together at night on weekdays looked a little something like this: "What time will you be home for dinner?"

"Oh, probably six thirty," I'd say.

"OK, honey, see you then."

At six thirty my cell would ring. Oh shit, I'd lost track of time. I'd let her call go to voice mail.

I'd walk in at 7:15 p.m. If any of the kids said or did anything I didn't like it would immediately set me off, and I'd act like an asshole. Brooding and selfish would be a spot-on description.

"Sorry babe, me and the kids were starving, so we ate without you," she'd say.

I don't blame her for becoming more and more distant. In her eyes, I'd lost interest, didn't have enough respect to show up on time for her delicious, nearly gourmet meals, and I was always in a mood.

After the kids went to bed, we'd head down into the finished daylight basement to watch TV or a movie together. We had a nine-foot ceiling, custom paint, frizze carpeting, and a sixteen-foot bar. In one corner was a beautiful stone fireplace next to daylight windows on the back wall, which overlooked the forty acres that friends call Bartopia. A sixty-three-inch plasma television hung to the left of the fireplace with nary a cord, DVD player, or DIRECTV box in sight…it was all controlled with infrared wavelengths and radio frequency.

Matching leather furniture surrounded the television: the recliner, then the loveseat, followed by the couch on the back wall. Behind the recliner was a custom-made eight-foot slate bed pool table with ridiculous one-hundred-dollar-bill emblazoned felt bumpers.

Stacey would sit in the recliner, and I would sit on the loveseat. We'd start a show or movie, and I would open a book, magazine, or newsletter to read. Or I'd scribble furiously on a notepad with a new idea for the real estate business.

If you've ever been in this situation, you know that Stacey was feeling alone and neglected. And I was too caught up my own mind and ego to even consider the effect.

The trip was my chance to make things right, but I didn't know that yet. After the guided tour of the resort, we stopped in an open-air restaurant, The Grill, and were immediately seated. The Hags insisted that we try an Iceberg. The Iceberg was a Corona Light served with a Margarita on top. It was delicious!

As we plowed through drink after drink we had very intellectual, even groundbreaking conversations. "Have you guys heard of fainting goats?" Casey quizzed.

"No, is that a band or something?" I replied.

"No, they're actual goats that literally faint when startled…just fall right over! You guys need to look 'em up on YouTube," she continued.

"Casey and I decided on a safe word," Jeff began. "If things get too carried away in the bedroom or hot tub or wherever, while we're here…we just scream out the safe word, and the other has to shut it down!"

"Ha ha ha, that's awesome! What's your safe word?" I asked, intrigued.

"Beef tenderloin!" Casey said with a roll of the eyes.

"Ha ha, why beef tenderloin?" Stacey laughed.

"Because beef tenderloin isn't a word you'd say on accident. When you say it, you really mean it!" Jeff explained.

"What's our word, honey?" Stacey asked.

"Uh, I don't know…maybe…Nuevo Uno Uno!"

We all laughed and continued to pound the Icebergs.

After dinner, we stumbled over to the outdoor bar where a band was jamming away on the stage. We got a table right in front of the makeshift dance floor in front of the small stage. We danced a couple of songs and continued to drink and dance. A Michael Jackson song came on in the middle of a story Stacey was telling Casey. I stood up and threw out a beautifully executed leg kick made famous by Michael himself. "C'mon!" I motioned to Stacey.

"Hold on. Let me finish this story," she replied.

When I'm drinking sometimes the smallest things will set me off. The dark passenger that resides inside of my head has a lot more influence over me when plied with alcohol.

I quickly sat back down and began to pout. He always justifies the shitty behavior. It seems like the thing to do at the time, so I typically go along with him. He, of course, is DP, the Dark Passenger.

Stacey continued her story, but was checking me out through the corner of her eye. She could probably tell by the body language. She'd certainly seen enough of it over the years. Ole jackass mode.

"You all right?" she asked. Arms crossed, just a head nod…an unconvincing yes. Drinks continued. Both of us were knee-walking drunk by this time.

The band continued with "Wonderful Tonight," by Eric Clapton. What a great song. Stacey stood and slowly made her way to the dance floor. We always dance to this song. I remained glued to the chair, arms crossed, eyes glazed. She motioned. I slowly shook my head with pursed lips...The Dark Passenger was running his mouth in my dumb drunken head.

She finally gave up, walked sadly back to our table, and grabbed her purse. "Let's call it a night." Casey and Jeff, huddled together with a plot to test their safe word, agreed.

We sauntered back to the room, Stacey walking a few paces in front with no plan to slow down. In the room after changing my clothes, I relieved my strained bladder, washed my hands and face, and brushed my teeth. Stacey was at the sink next to me, and we weren't speaking.

I climbed into bed, followed a couple minutes later by Stace. And she said...

"Should we get a divorce?"

I rolled over in disbelief to see her lying on her side facing me. Her head rested on one pillow, and she was hugging another. Her bloodshot eyes were filled with tears.

Before I had time to speak, the asshole spoke. "I don't know. Should we?"

What the hell kinda answer was that? I yelled in my head back at him!

I think I was in shock. We've been married for many years and the D word had never been uttered, not once! Not even jokingly.

This story continues in Chapter 39…

My life was about to change forever.

My business was about to change forever.

Both of these experiences inspired this book.

Enjoy.

CHAPTER 2

Who am I?

My name is Bart Vickrey, and last year I sold 250 homes while working no evenings, no weekends, and no Fridays...all while enjoying twelve weeks of vacation.

Although I carry nearly one hundred listings at any given time, I only went on two listings appointments last year. I showed houses to a total of one client, and that was because he was an old friend that I like spending time with.

I say this not to brag, although I am very proud.

The real estate business has been very good to me. I owe it a ton, but the job has taken its toll on me physically and emotionally, and it nearly cost me my marriage.

So, I write this book to accomplish a handful of very important things:

- To confess to you all of the mistakes I've made in my business and more importantly in my life. It seems counterintuitive to tell you about the mistakes, but believe me, if I can wave the warning flag ahead of time…hopefully you can avoid some of the heartbreak and anxiety that I've lived through…a lot of it self-induced.

- To show you all of the things that DID work for me! I'm going to share it all! This includes the discovery I've made that led to **"The Eighteen Steps to an Extra Million Dollars."** I know that sounds like late night infomercial bullshit. But I will give you all of the steps and describe in detail why each one is important. After reading through the list, you'll be thinking, Holy Shit, this is Pure Gold!

- To cross off becoming a bestselling author from my goal list. Back in about 1999 I started to consistently read books. Each year my goal would be to read a minimum of twelve. I never failed. At the beginning of this year, I upped the goal to twenty-four books. As I write this section (I started writing this book in June, but I'm writing the sections out of order) on August 19, I've already read twenty-six! With that said, my dream would be to read and write for a living. Maybe this is the start.

- To forever change your life for the better! I want to hear from you, "Bart, you have truly changed my life forever!" I'm not sure why my fragile psyche requires such backslapping, but it does. For many years, I've told my Bride, Stacey, that for some reason I have this unbridled desire to help positively impact the lives of others. You and I both know that one of my buyers or sellers is not going to approach me in a restaurant saying, "Hey Bart, I just wanted to tell you that you've changed my life forever!" It's not going to happen. So this book is my chance.

- To create a community of like-minded people. I've learned the hard way that money doesn't buy happiness, that things are just things, and that people, purpose, and experiences are the true path to happiness. How great would it be to have an outlet of like-minded people that we can communicate with? Most people err on the side of half-empty. They live with a scarcity mind-set and have no idea of the power and joy of giving. Today we change that…at least for us.

- To help catapult you to being a debt-free millionaire. One of the many mistakes I've made over the years was to fall for the scam of consumerism—the idea that we need fancy cars, huge homes, expensive jewelry, and always the next thing in order to be happy and fulfilled. The first thing I did when I started to make a lot of money was to spend a lot of money. Twice I've experienced credit card debt in excess of $30,000! Now I have none. No car payments. And my house will be paid off by the end of next year. Let's create a long-living legacy for you and your family starting now!

- To make you laugh, to make you cry, to make you believe. My story has many sad chapters. I'm still here to tell it, and to help you believe in YOU, because that's all you need (and this book of course!).

I will be sharing with you several stories from my childhood. Many of them contain sad situations involving my father. Please don't get the wrong impression. I love my dad with all my heart and have forgiven him for not being a good or even average father and for being the antithesis of a positive role model. I've accepted him exactly as he is.

As sad as some of the stories are, I know that countless people have had it far worse than I could ever imagine. So I desire no pity.

As Tony Robbins says, "You can live your life as an example or as a warning."

My Dad chose warning. I choose example.

CHAPTER 3

What to Expect

This will be unlike any real estate sales book you've ever read!

The book is filled mostly with stories. Half of the stories have nothing to do with real estate. You will, however, be entertained, which should be the underlying theme to all books. I read books to be entertained, educated, and inspired. This book will provide all three, albeit in an unconventional approach.

Most all of the stories are in the front of the book. Most all of the real estate sales strategies and tactics are in the back. If you are reading this on Amazon in the free *Look Inside* section and do not give a rat's can about the stories and just want the ways to improve your business...you can get them all for free at www.realestategoodlife.com. Just keep in mind that all of the stories created the author of the book. And the book is about to change your business and life forever.

I know this is probably crazy, but if you have any questions or just want to say hello you can e-mail me at bart@bartsellshouses.com. I invite your feedback and want to hear from you!

Every day we all wake up alone and afraid. We all struggle with doing the right things in the right order. We all suffer depression on some level. Many of us have been or are on the brink of financial disaster. We work in a business that's getting worse, not better. There are companies out there right now that are positioning themselves to eliminate us, or at least to greatly reduce our importance in the real estate transaction. They are creating a wedge between the consumer and us.

The answer is not to BUY more leads. The answer is to become indispensable, irreplaceable, an expert in your profession, and a linchpin within your community. The answer is to build a business that serves your life, not continue to have a job that controls your life.

We work and work in this business in order to provide for the people we love and cherish most in our lives. And in doing so, we create a job that steals us away from the very people we've set out to love and cherish!

The old way is over.

Welcome to *The Real Estate Good Life*!

CHAPTER 4

Big-Wheeled Mailbox Felons

When I was four years old, my family and I moved from a brand-new house on Robbie Lane in Valparaiso to a quad-level in Portage, Indiana.

Later I found out it was because my mother thought it was "a steal" that we couldn't pass up. It turned out to be a great move for my older brother Larry and me. A bunch of kids our age lived in the neighborhood, and we would all soon become fast friends. One of my new friends was Eric Walters. Eric was the same age as me and lived directly behind us with his older brother Danny.

One day when everybody else was at school, four-year-old Eric and I hopped on our big wheels and followed the mailman from house to house for nearly two blocks. The unsuspecting mailman would stop at each mailbox and make his delivery. We followed behind and withdrew each delivery and deposited the mail into the empty paint cans that we each had hanging from our handlebars.

After about twenty houses or so, our paint cans were filled to bursting, so we headed back to Eric's garage to inspect our haul. We had the mail all spread out over the garage floor when Eric's mom, Pat Walters, walked in.

"Oh my God! What in the world did you guys do? Do not touch another piece of mail!" Pat yelled. She wheeled quickly to her right and grabbed the receiver off the wall. I always thought it was awesome that they had a phone in the garage! Their garage also acted as the workshop and office of Eric's Dad, Gary. Gary was a Vietnam War veteran who had lost most of one of his legs in battle and now managed apartments for a local real estate tycoon.

Pat dialed furiously on the beige rotary phone. I still remember our old phone number in Portage, 762-9761. I didn't know at the time who she was calling, but looking back I think the long twists of the rotary dial should have clued me in!

"Sandi? Hi, it's Pat Walters! We have a big problem! I'm here with Bart and Eric, and they have stolen everyone's mail!"

C'mon, Pat! We didn't take everyone's mail. Our little paint cans only held about twenty families' worth.

"Right out of the mailboxes, I guess. They must have rode around on their big wheels from house to house! OK, I'll see you when you get here," Pat said.

Within a couple of minutes, my mother was standing next to Pat. They were both looming over Eric and me. We didn't really have a good answer for the questions they were asking, not even for the questions they seemed to ask repeatedly, "What were you going to with all this mail?" We hadn't thought through to the end game!

The four of us gathered up all the mail, and we hand delivered each piece to the appropriate mailbox. I tell you this story for no particular reason other than to share one of my earliest detailed memories. I can't help but think that I probably had bigger plans in mind than just collecting the mail for no reason. There may have been a business idea somewhere in there.

My mom owned a little beauty shop where she'd stand on her feet all day and doing ladies' hair. One day she was about to throw out a big binder full of blank business checks. Do you remember those long ones that had the ledger attached to the left of the check? You'd tear the check out and make a little note on the ledger as to its amount and recipient.

"Hey, can I have those?" I asked.

"Why do want these? They're no good. We canceled the account when we changed the business name," she said.

"I just want to play around with 'em."

"Sure. I guess. Just don't try to cash any!"

I grabbed 'em up and started using them for the make-believe companies that I'd created. One pretend business was Vickrey Entertainment. I'd written up a page long contract between me and a Vegas casino. It was for $1 million in exchange for live performances at the casino. When nobody was home, which was often, I'd fire up "You Dropped a Bomb On Me" by the Gap Band and put on a brilliant performance of singing and dancing.

The stage was the area with blue and yellow shag rug carpeting in front of the enormous mirror that hung from the wall separating the kitchen.

Before the show I'd pour myself a shot of Coca Cola, Pepsi, whatever we had, down it, and then take the stage.

My other companies were Wall Street Investments and Panther Car Company, and Vickrey Realty. For Wall Street Investments I would write down the names of ten or fifteen stocks, buy a bunch with my fake checks, follow their performance daily in the newspaper, and record my profits and losses in a notebook. For Panther Car Company I'd buy a few model car kits, you know the plastic ones you'd have to put together with the model glue that would get you a little buzzed. I would mix and match the parts and create my own designs and then sell them to GM and Ford. I also dominated the Pro Bowlers Tour in my kitchen and played in the NBA in the basement…both of which involved contracts, checks written from the old beauty shop checkbook, and fake cash I'd buy from Kaybee Toy and Hobby at the Southlake Mall. And the best part was that nobody in the family had any idea that I was a little tycoon running all of these imaginary enterprises!

Some people have a bunch of memories from a very early age, but not me. Most of my memories start at age four or five. I cannot for the life of me find one single legitimate memory of my dad living in the house with us as my dad, even though my parents didn't divorce until I was eight.

There are a handful of Dad-in-the-house memories, and he was probably living there as my dad at the time…but I think there were a lot of comings and goings and split-ups and separations in my parents' marriage for a long time before the final divorce.

I have one memory of a Saturday morning when I was probably around seven years old. I had this plastic bowling set that I would play with in the kitchen. I would set up the multicolored plastic pins and hurl the blue bowling ball that came with the set over and over again at the pins. I used the transition strip between the living room and kitchen carpet (yes, we had low pile carpeting in our kitchen) as the lane foul line.

On this particular morning my dad, Larry Sr., kept score for me from his seat at our snack bar. He wore faded Levi's and a tight white T-shirt, the kind Fonzi always wore. As he swilled cup after cup of black Folger's coffee and filled the room with smoke from his Winston's, he kept meticulous score of my bowling games.

I would check my score from time to time and would always admire how incredibly neat my father's handwriting was. This rare Dad-in-the-house memory ended abruptly. My brother, Larry Jr., had had his friend and catty-corner neighbor, Ron George, sleep over the night before. As I prepared for another probable strike on my makeshift bowling alley, I heard a disturbingly loud fart come from my brother's room followed immediately by hyena-like, high-pitched laughter. That was the end of that memory.

My brother, who is four-and-a-half years older than me, and as of this writing in his late forties, still finds farting a particularly hilarious subject.

Quick real-time update:

The family and I (Bride Stacey, oldest Madison, middle Maya, and youngest Bart II) were in Naples, Florida. We're visiting my mother, Aunt Vivian, and Granny Genevieve.

I made a quick trip to the bathroom, and when I returned there was an envelope with "Daddy" scrawled across the front. Inside was a Father's Day card from my Bride. My son, Bart II (we call him Deuce), and my mother had been sleeping over at Granny's and Aunt Viv's so that our sleeping arrangements could accommodate everyone. They just walked in, and Mother presented me with another Father's Day card. My oldest, Madison, then emerged from her and Maya's sleeping cave and handed me yet another card!

"What's this?" I asked, acting surprised.

"I don't know." Madison shrugged with a sheepish grin. Inside the kids wrote the following: "I love you, Dad!" This was from Deuce.

"Thank you for always being there for me and for telling crazy childhood stories," wrote Maya. "

You love, support, and inspire me. I'm so grateful that God, aliens, or whoever chose you to be my dad. You are the coolest Dad out there ☺, Your First Child," scribbled Madison.

I got a little choked up when I first read it, but I successfully played it off. The closeness with my children is so important to me because I never had that in my childhood. The feeling that I am really making a difference in their lives give me joy beyond words. My reason for everything I do, both business and personal, is for the love of my family.

CHAPTER 5

Dad's Sixteen-Year-Old Girlfriend

It was June of 1980, and Dad was picking Larry and me up for a visit. In the divorce decree, the court ruled that Dad would have custody every other weekend and a couple of weeks in the summer.

He pulled up in his 1973 Corvette, black with red racing stripes and big chrome side pipes. It wasn't exactly a family car, but our friends all thought it was pretty cool.

Dad had a girl in the car with him. She had raven-black hair and tan skin and was very petite, probably around five foot two. She was cute in a trashy kind of way, and really young. "Hi, guys. I'm Tracy. It's nice to meet you!"

"Get in, boys. Bart, you sit on Larry's lap while we drop Tracy off." Larry and I looked at each other in disbelief.

A Corvette and four passengers don't mix! Dad drove, trashy Tracy rode in the middle, sitting on the center console, and I sat on Larry's lap. We looked like a couple of weirdos stuffed in that car! As we drove off, I noticed a pair of red panties hanging from the rearview mirror. How embarrassing! Could this visit have started any more awkwardly?

"How old are you guys?" Tracy quizzed. "I'm nine!" said the cute one. "I'm thirteen, gonna be fourteen in September," Larry begrudged. "Oh my God, we're almost the same age, Larry! I'm sixteen!

I felt Larry's body stiffen with the horrifying news. Larry had always taken the separation and divorce of our parents much harder than me. He would never accept another woman, certainly not some brazen hussy that was less than three years older than he was!

Ha! I just looked up "brazen hussy" on Google to make sure I was spelling it right…and Paris Hilton showed up in the search as one of the images!

The horror (no pun intended) didn't end there. As we drove out of Portage and into Lake Station, I figured we were dropping Tracy off at her house. But noooo, we pulled up to River Forest High School. Dad stopped the car, got out, and kissed his lady good-bye.

What the heck is going on around here? I thought. After a few awkward moments Larry asked, "Does Tracy work at the school?" "No, she's in summer school," Dad said nonchalantly.

We then drove up Central Avenue in Lake Station to Long John Silver's. I ordered the chicken plank and fries basket, and Larry had the same. We chomped down our lunch and tried to have a normal conversation with Dad, as he dumped Visine into each bloodshot eye.

Larry and I loved Long John Silver's back in the day, so it became Dad's go-to move when he had to spend time with us.

After lunch we loaded back into the two-seater and made tracks back home. He dropped us off and left to a chorus of Larry and me yelling, "Light 'em up!" Dad then proceeded to smoke the tires of the Corvette without regard for any of the children running amok in the neighborhood!

Sadly, we never saw Tracy, the raven-haired hussy, again. I hope she made it through summer school! There's no doubt she turned out to be an upstanding and productive member of society.

Memories like these make for good stories, maybe bad, depending on perspective. I look at them all as experience and the beginnings of a future skillset. Learning to get along with Tracy in that moment can be deciphered as a skillset, right?

When asked the <u>one</u> secret to real estate success, I always answer the same. That one secret is rapport. The ability to build genuine rapport with people will always deliver an advantage. Rapport opens doors. Whether it's the client, appraiser, loan officer, or the agent on the other side of the negotiation… start with rapport.

CHAPTER 6

Haggard Whores and Conway Twitty

O ne night I was getting ready for bed and the doorbell rang. It was my dad, and he was drunk. He often visited drunk in those early years of my parents' separation and eventual divorce.

As a boy, I didn't understand why my dad acted this way. It was hard enough to not have both parents in the house, to overhear arguments, to be let down, disappointed, and downright heartbroken, but being a little man middleman just wasn't fair at all.

Later, as I matured, and eventually discovered more details, I completely understood that my mother virtually had no choice but to divorce my father. Believe it or not, I have never really had hard feelings toward my dad, never much anger, and certainly no hatred. I have learned that he simply has demons. For many years these demons got the better of him. And still, long after he's kicked the drinking habit, these demons have rendered him a near recluse inside his trailer in Portage, Indiana.

"Hi, Dad."

"Hi, son. Whatcha doing?" he slurred.

"Oh, just getting ready for bed," I reported.

"Came by to see ya. Can I come in?" I was hoping he'd stay in his car like so many other times before. He wanted to come in this time. Maybe he knew another man was there? His eyes were glassy, and his body smelled as if it were ensconced in alcohol. Fumes were escaping his pores from the countless drinks he had likely swilled.

We lived in a quad-level at 5551 Lark Avenue in Portage, Indiana. The main level consisted of a foyer, a family room with brick fireplace that was converted from a one-car garage, a three-quarter bathroom, and, at the rear of the house, the master bedroom. Dad followed me upstairs from the foyer as I reluctantly agreed to his visit.

We passed by the living room with its flamboyant decor, yellow and blue shag carpeting accentuated the furry yellow couch and loveseat. In front of the couch were two hand-painted ceramic elephants about three feet in diameter each. Perched atop the elephants was a glass coffee table. My friends and I would inadvertently run our legs into this coffee table several times over the years. You couldn't see the damn thing!

Sitting on the overstuffed yellow couch on this night was my mother and her date, Conway Twitty. I still couldn't tell you his actual name. I just know that Larry and I nicknamed him Conway Twitty. Twitty was a popular country singer at the time. His best song was probably, "Hello Darlin'." Conway Twitty had a big, robust, helmetlike hair-do…and so did this guy. So, thusly named.

I immediately felt the tension as we walked by on our way to the kitchen. Oh, I forgot to mention that my dad had a pistol holstered at his hip. So I asked him about the gun, making conversation and feigning interest. I never did get into guns. In fact, I have never even fired a real gun. "Cool gun. If you shot it right now, how far would it go?" I asked. I didn't know what kind of questions to ask about a damn gun!

"The bullet would go through this jar [pointing to the jar of Orville Redenbacher popcorn sitting on the burnt orange snack bar we were sitting at], through the dining room wall, through the Wilson's house (next door), and into the Mucha's living room!" he said proudly.

"Wow," I said, acting like I gave a shit.

Dad then started saying things a little louder so that Mom and Twitty could hear. Stuff like "I'm still in love with your Mother" and "When I move back in!" That's when Mom came around the corner from the living room through the dining room.

"Larry, can I talk to you in the hall?" she said.

"Sure, honey," he stated.

I didn't hear what she said to him, but she must have asked him to leave.

"I'm here to visit my son, Bart. I'm not leaving unless he wants me to leave!" he said.

He then peeked his head around the corner and asked me, "Bart, do you want me to leave?"

I actually just got tears in my eyes thinking about it as I sit here writing. It's just not fair to put a little boy in that situation. Just as I teared up now, my eyes filled then too. I remember desperately not wanting to cry. I couldn't answer his question without bawling, so I just stared at the countertop trying to regain my composure.

Even in his drunken state, my dad must have sensed my fragile emotional state. "Come on, son. Walk me out," he said. I was instantly relieved. As we walked from the kitchen through the near end of the living room toward the stairs to the foyer, my dad stared at Conway Twitty. He hugged me good-bye. He always hugged me very tight when he was drunk. Looking back now, I feel sorry for him. I'm sure he wanted to be a better father. He just didn't have it in him at the time.

So there's a little more to this episode. Ole Conway Twitty used to be our next-door neighbor when we lived on Robbie Lane in Valparaiso. He and his wife, Gwen, had the nicest house in the neighborhood with an in-ground pool and a pond on the property, the whole deal. While living on Robbie Lane, my mother had a beauty shop in the basement. Gwen was a regular customer. She reminded me of a female Liberace. She was old, smoked long cigarettes, and wore tons of jewelry and too much perfume. Apparently, sometime after we moved to Portage, Gwen and Twitty's marriage dissolved. I'm not sure how or why my mother stayed in contact with Twitty, but now they were dating.

A couple of nights later, Dad showed up drunk again. Thankfully, Larry was home to help take some of the pressure off me. "Hey, boys, come out and take a ride in my new car!" he said. I still remember that I was wearing my Star Wars pajamas. I never did like that slit in the front of the pajama pants, right in front of my junk! I guess it's there to pee through, but I never did use it. I mean, what was I supposed to do, reach through that slot, somehow finagle my weenie out of my underwear and then thread it through the opening? That seemed absurd—especially when all I had to do was, with one fell swoop, grab the waistband of both the *Star Wars* pajamas and the Fruit of the Loom tighty whities and stretch them down, thus exposing the wiener now prepared for unobstructed urination.

Larry and I put on our shoes and ran outside to the driveway. Sitting there was a beautiful, brand new, pearl white Cadillac Fleetwood. You know, the kind of Cadillac that's the size of a pontoon boat? We piled in the back, Dad hopped in the driver's seat, and do you know who was sitting all smiles and smeared lipstick in the passenger seat? Ole sweetheart Gwen! Are you kidding me? Gwen seemed ancient! Atop her bird-size head she wore a teased wig that was puffy from using too much hairspray. She always seemed to be snapping gum and getting red lipstick on her teeth, and she was never without a long, skinny brown More cigarette.

We took an uncomfortable spin around the block while Gwen peppered us with stupid questions. "Do you guys like school? What grade are you in? We should all go out to dinner! What's your favorite food?" she babbled. Shut the hell up, you old hag! Take me home and let me out of this Corinthian leather, cheap perfume, alcohol, cigarette smoke, and Aqua Net smelling hell ride. I have school tomorrow!

What if my life did not include made for tv moments? If I had lived in a household intact. Who knows? Maybe I'd be like most, average or mediocre. That's how I have to look at it. Glass half full. The experiences I've had unique. My shape was formed by every episode. Not to be looked upon with sorrow, but as having survived. Intact. Mostly unscathed.

CHAPTER 7

Bring Your Kid to the Bar Day!

D ad was late picking me up that Saturday. He arrived in the black Corvette with the red racing stripe. Plumes of cigarette smoke billowed out of the car when Shirley opened the passenger side door.

"You can sit on my lap sweetie," Shirley said.

Shirley was midthirties with raven black hair, pale white skin, and a ruddy face. Her eyes were old and tired, as if they'd seen more than her age would suggest. Shirley was an "entertainer" Dad told me. Later he'd use the description "professional dancer." Truth was Shirley danced all right; she danced naked! My dad's serious girlfriend and soon to be third wife (fourth marriage, more on that later) was a stripper at one of the seediest strip joints in the area, Scuttlebutt Lounge.

She was also the ostracized aunt of one of my friends at school. I endured some ribbing on account of that relationship.

As it turned out I really got to like Shirley. She was very sweet, a genuinely nice and caring person. But on this Saturday morning I barely knew her, and yet I sat awkwardly on her leather-covered lap. I kind of got the feeling that I was not part of their original plans that day. Dad probably forgot all about it being his weekend to "have" me.

"Well, what do you think?" Dad said to ole hot pants.

"It doesn't matter to me. We can do whatever you want," she said.

"Let's just go over for a while," Dad quipped.

"OK, sure," Shirley said accommodatingly. They then peppered me with the requisite questions about school, basketball, etc. for about twenty minutes until we arrived at a familiar sight: Bud's Bar in Lake Station, Indiana. Bud's was a dark, seedy watering hole in a once popular small town. It was the kind of place was so dark you never knew the time of day outside. The place had a stable of regulars. Looking back now, I picture the bar scene from *Star Wars*. Creeps, trolls, hunchbacks, and goblins kept Bud's Bar in business.

"Let's go in for a little while. What do you say, Bart?" my dad said as if I should be excited.

"Uh, OK," I said. It was around 11:00 a.m. on a Saturday morning, Even my young brain found it a little disconcerting to be: A. Going to a bar at this time of day? And B. Dragging your ten-year-old part-time son with you? And C. Wearing leather pants. I mean, who the hell really wears leather pants? Although, I still laugh when I think of the *Friends* episode when Ross wears leather pants. He's at a girl's apartment, uses the bathroom, and then can't get his leather pants back up. It's a hilarious scene.

Once inside we joined my Uncle Dale's table. He had some trollop on his arm. Dale was now recently divorced from Aunt Liz (whom I really liked). His friend Dave Jenne also had a young jewel by his side. Dave had been married to my mother's sister, my Aunt Vivian. He was also the father of my cousin Dawn, who grew up basically like my little sister. Many profound marital influences in my early life and none of them were good.

They all acted like I was a welcomed guest and asked me questions that I had already answered whilst stuffed into Dad's Corvette on the way over. They soon forgot I was there and continued with their drinking and carrying on. As I was looking over this band of misfits, I quickly noted that every single one of them was smoking. We were literally enveloped in smoke. And it wasn't just the family members and hussies sitting at the table that were puffing the fags, it was every single person in the bar.

I sat there for what seemed an eternity but probably was like an hour and a half, maybe two. Then I just started crying. I want to blame the smoke as I did then. But it wasn't the smoke; it was my circumstance.

Sadness over the barely recognizable memory of my parents' marriage, sadness over the selfish thought of what I was missing while holed up in this crummy bar. All my neighborhood friends were likely outside enjoying the sunshine, probably playing whiffle ball or pickle together. "Larry, he's crying!" Shirley said, concerned.

"Son, what's wrong?" Dad questioned.

"Uh, I think it's all the smoke. My eyes keep watering," I whimpered.

At the time I thought maybe I had pulled it off. I hoped they believed the story—and the smoke was indeed bothering and burning my eyes, but the tears flowed from a different place.

"Ten minutes and we'll leave, OK, son?" said Dad.

"Uh, sure," I uttered disappointedly. C'mon, Dad, are you serious? Not only do you have me at a bar with your stripper girlfriend on a Saturday, but now I'm crying! And you're still not ready to leave?

Another twenty minutes passed. I'd stopped crying on the outside, but the interior was still in shambles.
"Dad? I'm gonna wait outside," I said.
"Oh Larry, let's get that poor boy out of here," Shirley genuinely offered. Dad snuffed out his Winston, drained the last of his drink, and finally stood up.

We stuffed back into the two-seater and pulled around to the side of the building. At the drive-through window Dad ordered "one more for the road, a Seven and Seven." The drink came out disguised in one of those little Styrofoam coffee cups. It even had a lid and one of those red mixing straws to add more camouflage to the drive-home beverage of choice.

We made it back to Dad's trailer in Portage in about ten minutes. It was early afternoon by then, and I was hungry. Shirley whipped up a hot batch of fish sticks and fries from the freezer that I enjoyed in the tiny living room while staring at the TV. Dad and Shirley retreated to "my" bedroom and fired up the ole ColecoVision for some *Donkey Kong*, beer drinking, and chain smoking.

After my nutritious lunch, I joined them in the cramped bedroom for a few rounds with the big ape. Why did they call it Donkey Kong anyway? He wasn't a donkey; he was a big, dumb ape! I really like donkeys, especially miniature ones! I always tell Stacey that we're going to get a miniature donkey for the backyard and name him Don Vickrey, middle name Key.

The smoke was getting thick in the tiny game room. Normally I would have stayed the night as planned, but the overwhelming urge just hit me: I had to escape!

"Dad, can you take me home?" I asked.

Dad looked shocked when he answered, "Well, what's wrong, son? We don't have to play this game anymore. We can do whatever you want."

I lied, "I think I just want to go home. I'm not feeling very good." I felt fine physically, but emotionally I just wasn't feeling it.

"Uh, sure, if you really want to go, but I wish you'd stay," Dad pleaded.

He drove me home, leaving Shirley to prepare for her "professional" dancing gig. When I got home it was turning dusk. Larry was in the front yard playing catch with Ron George. "Thought you were staying the night?" he asked. The "not feeling good" charade continued. I raced inside while Larry and Ron talked to Dad. I threw my pillow and gym bag into my room and was back on the streets before Dad made it to the end of the block. Weekend saved. Memory, unfortunately, preserved.

Patience is a virtue. So they say. Despite my desperate need to get out of that bar, I hung in there. Not sure why at the time. Just did. Remained patient. Now I get to look back and make my own choice on how these stories play out. Powerful feeling. I can blame my circumstance or I can credit them for creating the me I am.

Patience and perseverance have a powerful, if not magical effect on the roadblocks we all encounter. Hang in. Stay the course. Exhausting, burdensome, and grueling barriers seem to vanish, when you do.

CHAPTER 8

Pull my finger

"Hey Pal, pull my finger!" These were the first words uttered to me by him. He was my mom's new boyfriend, John. He stood about five feet eleven inches and was a little fluffy in the midsection. Not fluffy in today's almost-everyone-is-fat standards but fluffy in 1980 standards.

I was nine years old so, of course, I pulled his finger. An eardrum rattling percussion then exploded out of John's backside, followed by a belly-deep chuckle that made me immediately like him! He was kind of a strange-looking fellow with big, wild eyes but how many dudes have the thought process required to blow off a huge fart upon meeting the girlfriend's son for the first time? Not many I would guess.

Most people put on kind of a charade upon first meeting. And some even try to maintain said charade throughout a relationship. Give me someone that's authentic any day over some phony bologna!

John was certainly authentic. He was thirty-two years old back in 1980 and sold insurance for Prudential. He lived in a trailer on the other side of town in Portage and drove an orange 1977 Monte Carlo with a white vinyl top.

Once it became evident that John and Mom were serious, he pulled Larry and I aside one day for a little chat. He basically told us that he loved our mother and wanted to marry her. "Boys, there will always be a Cadillac in the driveway and a pool in the backyard!" he told us.

Sounded good to us! We gave our consent.

The night before John and Mom were to get married, they had a little gathering at the house with a couple of John's siblings, his mom and dad, who were in town for the wedding, Aunt Viv, and a couple close friends.

As the night wore on, the front door flung open and there stood my dad. He didn't even knock. He just walked right in, made a beeline for the family room, and collapsed on the couch. He was three sheets to the wind! Drunk as a skunk. He passed out face down in the couch with the brown grip of a .38 revolver just above his beltline.

There was an initial shock-and-awe scramble with people saying, "What should we do?" "Someone call the cops!" and "Bart, go to your room!" Then my mom grabbed the gun out of his waistband and put it away. I guess the plan now was to let him sleep it off. Reluctantly, everyone went back up to the second floor where the small party continued. Larry and I were allowed to come back into the family room. We were watching TV out of the corner of one eye and keeping surveillance on dad with the other. Awkward is an understatement to describe the way we were feeling.

It was already weird enough that on the very next day our mother was getting married to John. The marriage would put an end to any day-dreaming fantasies of our parents ever getting back together, and when you're nine years old that's a little sad. But now to have good ole Dad passed out on the couch with a gun...Larry and I didn't know what the hell to do!

We were laughing our way through a rerun of the sitcom *Soap* on ABC when suddenly he stirred. He sat up abruptly coughed and did a little rid-the-cobwebs shake of his head. With that, Dad stood staggered through the foyer and was out the door before Larry or I could utter a word.

We both ran upstairs to report the goings-on. "Hey, Mom! Dad just woke up and then left!" Larry yelled.

"Did he say anything to you guys?" Mom asked.

"No, he just left!" Larry offered.

I'm not sure that my mom ever did give that gun back, nor did Larry or I ever bring up the wild and hardly believable visit to my dad or anyone else for that matter.

Everyone survived and made it to the wedding the following day. The ceremony was at the house, very informal. As this was both John and Mom's second marriage they just wanted to keep it simple.

The two most indelible memories from the wedding day are the terrible live music playing on the patio in the backyard, and the fact that I downed sixteen ten-ounce bottles of Pepsi during the reception.

We filled two garbage cans with beverages on the brown sectional couch where the night before my dad had lain passed out. One contained what seemed to be an infinite supply of Pepsi! I loved Pepsi back then! Sixteen bottles in a night is still, by far, a record for me!

The live music wailing away in the background was an eclectic group of nearly talentless musicians. My cousin Bobby Clark was on guitar and lead vocals, Larry was on guitar, and our neighbor Ron George was on drums.

They called themselves the Bonds Brothers Band. Our nickname for Cousin Bobby was Bonds after the professional baseball player Bobby Bonds. Later Bobby's son Barry would enter Major League Baseball and break the all-time home run record.

The group had never practiced together and only had a three-song repertoire. All three songs were brutally murdered during their set. Rumor had it that the horrific music could be heard down at Myers Elementary, which was about half a mile down the road.

The music was shut down about an hour into the set when the Paulsons called the Police. The Paulsons were the first house on the right from our backyard. Their kids went to a Catholic school and the mom, Sandy Paulson, called us public schoolers and always had it out for me and Larry. This was probably because her son, Tommy, never did fit in with our click of fairly normal, athletic, and somewhat mischievous boys, and that may have been the case because Tommy was a dick!

The funny thing is that Sandy Paulson and I ended up at the same real estate office in 1998 when I first got my license. She used to tell my wife all the time how chubby I was as a kid! It didn't matter how many times I told her she had me mistaken for some other neighborhood kid, she stuck to her story. Crazy old bat, I weighed barely more than the wind as a kid!

To be honest I must have completely repressed the memory of the dad incident from the night before the wedding. It wasn't until I was discussing this book with my mother that she brought up, "Remember when your Dad showed up the night before John and I got married…" More and more revealed itself once the memory was awakened, and I started to write about it.

I've got to hand it to my mom though. For all the shit my dad pulled during their marriage, subsequent separation, and then divorce, she never did talk bad about him around us boys.

Despite the overwhelming desire to trash talk or bad mouth my competitors, I've always refrained. My philosophy likely stems from the example my mother set for me.

My team has all been trained in the same way. Never talk bad about your competition in front of a client or prospective client. No need. Be your best, do your best.

CHAPTER 9

John M. Childress

He would make funny faces behind my mother as she tried to discipline my brother and me.

He was white collar but tried to act blue collar. He once bought a chainsaw and cut down all of the shrubs between us and the next-door neighbor. He was wearing Sansabelt pants and a white dress shirt. Because he didn't know how to put the oil and gas in properly, his shirt was streaked with oil by the time he was done.

A few days later he tried to drag the stumps and roots out of the ground with his Toyota Tercel.

He had quotes my brother and I still use till this day!

- "Get off your dead legs and dying ass!"
- "She's a double bubble off." (I still don't know exactly what that means.)
- "Give me five minutes, Pal." (He called everyone Pal and always asked for five-minute breaks when he tried to play basketball with us in the driveway.)

- "I'll just eat bread!" he said to my mother one night when he came home drunk hours late for dinner. We'd already eaten.
- "With a touch of luck…" He'd say often, attached to anything with an outcome.

I can go on with the quotes, but maybe it's time for some stories.

On August 1, 1980, John became my stepdad. From day one his act was comedic. His promise to my brother and me was a Cadillac in the driveway and a pool in the backyard. We never got the pool. He did buy a Cadillac once, but it was maybe the worst Cadillac model ever produced—the Cimarron. What a crappy excuse for a Cadillac! The car was basically a Cavalier with Cadillac badges.

We had a water valve and pipe in our front yard that rose about six inches from the ground. John didn't like it. So one day, in his suit and tie, he tried to beat it into the ground with a sledgehammer! I'm not sure why he thought this was a good idea, but leave it to John! The pipe broke underground causing water to flood the yard. We had to call the water department out to fix the damage.

"Do you know what happened?" they asked John.

"No, but I did see an old lady back her car into our yard the other day," he lied with a straight face.

With that same chainsaw mentioned before, he went on a rampage once. We had a wood-burning fireplace, and John wanted to stock up on wood for the winter. He called everyone he knew to find out if they had any trees they needed cut down. One guy told him he was building a house on a wooded lot. The builder had all the trees knocked down, but they were still on the property. John could have all the wood he wanted!

He literally spent every Saturday and Sunday for a month gathering wood from that lot. Larry and I would split it when he'd drop it off, while he headed for another load. We then were instructed to stack the wood along the fence line that the Walters had installed between the two yards.

The Walters had a new pool, so the city required a fence. They put up a six-foot chain link and then wove in different colored vinyl strips for privacy. You remember those dopey fences! It looked horrific!

We stacked and stacked and stacked! By the time we were done, John had cut up enough wood to go from one end of our backyard to the other, stacked five feet high! There was still a ton of wood left when we sold the house in 1986.

One of the many times that my brother had clogged up the toilet, John had had enough! He ran into the family room where Larry and I were watching football, "Listen Jumbo Dumbo (that's what he started calling my brother when he began putting on slabs of muscle in high school), if you clog up the goddam toilet one more time, you're going to have to shit in a garbage can in the backyard!" I still tease my brother about that whenever he says he needs to use my bathroom.

I do still have a recurring nightmare caused by Larry within this context. There I was on a Saturday morning in the family room on the dumpy old brown sectional minding my own business, enjoying me some Scooby-Doo…and in flashed Larry laughing like a hyena!

He was armed with something! I couldn't tell what it was through my peripheral vision. With a whir and a slosh I was suddenly struck squarely in the face with a still-dripping plunger! My entire face froze in horror! It was as if I had been blasted with a Taser, and my movement was rendered still, my thoughts scrambled.

Suddenly I came to, regained my breath, and thought intersected with circumstance. "I've just been plunged!" I thought, mortified. My face was moist and puckered. I knew that that could only mean one thing! The diabolical weapon used in this sibling attack was indeed a freshly deployed toilet plunger!

I belted out a high-pitched squeal and began sobbing like a new-born baby! In rushed mother. "Larry! What the hell are you doing?" she screamed. Doubled over in uncontrollable laughter, Larry was no match for the quick catlike movements of mother, who immediately disarmed my assailant and dispensed a series of furious plunger blows to his now startled clown-like face.

"You got it in my mouth!" he yelled and ran out of the room, the fresh toilet water leaving an indelible impression on his wispy, mustached face.

In my entire childhood I went on three vacations. Four if you count the time I went to New Orleans with mom and John for an insurance conference.

I remember we stayed at the Hyatt Regency downtown. We visited the French Quarters, Bourbon Street, and some old mansion. During the conference they'd leave me in the hotel room. I had my jam box with me and was armed with a handful of my favorite cassettes.

The second they'd leave I'd throw in Midnight Star's new album *No Parking on the Dance Floor* and play the song "Freak-a-zoid" over and over again. You know the song, "Freakazoids...robots...please report! Freakazoids...robots...please report to the dance floor!" The voice had a mechanical robot accent. I'd then sneak out of the room, ride the elevator down, and spend hours in the arcade. I'd love to know how many quarters I shoveled into *Q*Bert*, *Dig Dug*, and *Donkey Kong*!

I tie two other memories directly to that trip. One is that it was the second to the last week of school and I missed Wednesday, Thursday, and Friday. On that Thursday we had our school awards ceremony.

It was the first year that one student took home both big athletic awards. Unfortunately the student was in New Orleans. The awards were Athletic Scholarship and Athletic Mental Attitude. There was one other award I missed that day also. The crowd roared when they announced my name for perfect attendance, and of course I wasn't there!

The other memory I did not witness. But the story was embarrassingly repeated over the years. John and Mom were entering the conference room lobby on the first morning. John recognized a fellow Prudential Insurance agent from the Chicagoland region.

"Hey Reggie. How ya doing pal?" John asked.

"Good John, how are you?" Reggie replied, standing in front of his wife and four children.

"Looks like you brought the whole tribe with ya!" John observed.

"Uh…yeah, uh, this is my wife…" Reggie went on to introduce his wife and kids by name.

Reggie was black. According to my mother, he was immediately taken off guard by John's comment. John being John had no idea what he said could possibly be construed as anything but friendly.

The other three trips were actual vacations, two of which I recollect as only vague memories. When Larry and I were around the ages of nine and four, Dad and Mom took us to the Smokey Mountains in Tennessee and the Wisconsin Dells.

With John and Mom, we drove down to Florida and stayed with John's parents. Being in the back of the orange 1977 Monte Carlo for twenty-one hours with Larry was no picnic. We would take turns lying down, one on the backseat and the other on the floorboards. Talk about uncomfortable! Larry was bigger and stronger, so I spent a lot of time on the floorboards that road trip. To top it off Larry was farting all over the place!

The stay at John's parents was fairly uneventful. We did visit Disney World for my first time ever, but I don't think we even stayed long enough to enjoy the fireworks. I certainly don't remember it if we did. We also visited John's cousin who lived nearby in Kissimmee. It was the Fourth of July and they were having a cookout. Larry and I were entertaining ourselves with some low-end fireworks. We got bored, so we started throwing lit sparklers into the field behind John's cousin's house.

"Fire!" someone yelled! I can still picture the scene. The weed-riddled and unkempt field was located at the end of the property on the other side of a farm style fence. The smoke began to billow and the weeds were suddenly ablaze!

Everything in me tightened! At this moment nobody at the party had any idea who or what triggered the inferno. Everyone began to scramble, and we formed a human assembly line. We tried to deliver buckets of water to the flames, but John's cousin's backyard was long and narrow like a bowling alley, probably a full acre in size.

The garden hose was stretched out taunt, turned on full blast, and the operator was filling anything that would hold water. Several buckets, several trips, repeated dousing…it wasn't enough! The fire found nearby dried brush and weeds to mate with.

My heart was pounding as we tried desperately to contain the fire. Thoughts of burning down the neighborhood and possible incarceration raced through my head!

Then the sirens. Oh crap! I thought. Jail it is!

A gravel service road ran parallel to the property. The bright red fire truck arrived in haste, and three guys in full gear bolted from the truck. Within two minutes the inferno was doused!

John and his cousin stood off about twenty feet from where Larry and I stared apprehensively. Their lips were moving, but all we could hear were hushed mumblings. Then one of the firefighters held up a burned-out sparkler. John and his cousin immediately turned their attention directly to Larry and me.

"Boys, come over here," John instructed. He always called us boys. Still does. "Were you guys throwing sparklers over the fence?" he asked.

"Yes," was all I could get out.

"You guys have to be more careful. One of the sparklers you threw away must have been so hot it started the fire," John went on.

Holy cow! I thought. They have no idea we were throwing them still sparkling over the fence!

We got away with that one. Years later while reliving old stories Larry and I confessed to Mom.

On the long car ride home I couldn't wait till we got to Tennessee. John promised us on the way down that on the way home we'd stop for some fireworks. In the early eighties fireworks were illegal in Indiana. So locally all we could get our hands on was smoke bombs, sparklers, snakes, and snappers.

In Tennessee we could get all the good stuff! At least all the stuff that we really wanted. The cheap stuff like bottle rockets, witch whistles, and firecrackers. Larry and I each got four gross (the unit was called a gross and numbered 144 in total) of bottle rockets, one gross of witch whistles, and a brick of Black Cat firecrackers. A brick held eighty packs, with sixteen firecrackers per pack. It was the best part of the trip!

We returned home and began to terrorize the neighborhood with our illegal goods! My neighbor Ronnie Howerton and I tried dozens of firecracker experiments. What could a firecracker blow up? That was our simple query. Not much, it turned out.

Some of the kids, like Joseph Poirier who lived across the street, weren't allowed around the fireworks. Looking back, I can see that that was probably a wise parenting move. I was about eleven years old at the time, wielding illegal explosives.

One day Mr. Howerton who lived next door to the Poiriers was in his backyard minding his own business. I slowly snuck around the corner between Joseph and Ronnie's house. Ken had his back to me. I couldn't resist!

I held the entire pack of explosive kitties tightly in my left hand. In my right was a red, plastic, oval-shaped fire-making device with the letters

B I C engraved near the top. With the hard pressure exerted by my right thumb onto the flint roller, the flame jumped to life. I inched the twisted wick closer and closer to the flame. Suddenly sparks jumped from the papered wick, and I tossed the whole lot in what felt like slow motion to green grass situated directly behind my unsuspecting victim…and then ran like hell.

SSSzzz…pop…pop…pop…poppopopop…several more cracks and pops. A loud shriek, a startled yell! Boo yeah! I thought.

As I now half jogged near the far end of Joseph's front yard…all at once he was on my heels! "Holy crap!" I yelled inside as I tried to turn on the jets! It was too late. He had me. He swiftly grabbed hold of my elbow with his left hand and thundered my rear with a hurried *whap! whap! whap!*

Oh My God! I just got spanked by Mr. Howerton! It all happened so suddenly and was such a surprise that as he quickly offered three or four decisive but far from violent smacks to my buttocks, my bladder made its own decision! It decided to release the hounds! The hounds being any and all urine that was currently housed in said bladder.

Yeah! Not only had I been publicly spanked by Ronnie's dad, but now this once playful event had turned into a pee party in my pants. OK, I wasn't wearing pants. They was actually navy-blue short, shorts that went as far as mid-thigh and had two white stripes on either side.

I quickly regained composure and without saying a word I went to my room and stripped off my pee-soaked tighty whities and favorite shorts. Nobody ever brought up the pee pants, so I think I'm the only who knew, and only two or three neighborhood friends witnessed the beat down. In fact, I'm not sure I've ever told anyone about the pants peeing part!

Anyway, that evening at dinner I told the story of being spanked by Mr. Howerton. Larry thought it was hilarious! My mom yelled at me. John finished dinner and then marched right over the Howerton's where he gave ole Kenny a talking to.

I thought it was cool at the time that John stood up for me. The truth is, I completely deserved the spanking and then some!

It turned out that as much as John was fun and entertaining for me and Larry, Mom had married another alcoholic. The big difference was that John was a happy drunk, and Dad was a violent one. Not that that's consolation for Mother, or something she should have had to settle for.

CHAPTER 10

Another Divorce?

It was Monday June 5, 1989, two days after my high school graduation open house. My mother and stepfather said they needed to speak with me.

I was sure it had to do with the beer my friends and I had smuggled from the open house, which we then drank after everyone had gone home, but I was wrong.

"Bart," my mother said. "John and I are getting a divorce."

"Uh, why?" I said feeling confused.

"We decided that after all these years, we are better off as friends," Mom said.

"But I want you to know that you're welcome back here any time you want, pal" John said with a smile.

"What does that mean? Are we moving?" I said looking at Mom. Now they had my attention! A divorce announcement is one thing, lol. But moving, no way!

"We talked it over, and John wants to keep the house, so you and I are going to find a new place," Mom said with an isn't-this-great tone. No, this is far from great, I thought to myself.

We then packed up and moved across town to my Aunt and Uncle's double-wide trailer located in the Pleasant Valley mobile home park in Portage, Indiana. It took me like two weeks before I even told my girlfriend Misty that I had moved and another day or two after that before I told her it was to a trailer. I was embarrassed to the point of depression!

My bedroom was the living room couch. Oh the humanity, I thought! I remember going to sleep on the couch each night that summer thinking two things:

1. How early was Uncle Ray going to wake me up this time? Ray was a drywaller and woke up at the butt-crack of dawn and rattled around the trailer with no regard for my sleeping arrangements. I'm pretty sure Ray was as thrilled with me living there as I was.
2. There's got to be more in store for me than this? Sleeping on a couch in a trailer and having my feet attacked at night by a rabid wiener dog named Muffin was not how my life is supposed to play out!

Something changed in me that summer. Sleeping on that couch, being bullied by that damn wiener dog, experiencing the end of a marriage. It was a small change, but small changes add up.

That summer was the beginning of my awakening. That summer matured me just enough to see that if I wanted a different circumstance, then I was responsible for delivering it!

The same is true for your real estate business. You cannot blame your broker, you cannot blame the franchise or the company you're associated with, you cannot blame your spouse for not supporting you. The results are up to you!

If you want to know the absolutely positively unadulterated SECRET to success in life and the real estate business then keep reading down to the P.P.S. It's only two words long, but it's guaranteed to better your life and business forever!

P.S. My parents divorced when I was young. And between them they've accumulated six failed marriages. Just FYI, lol!

P.P.S. Daily Habits. Positive daily habits aligned with any particular goal will deliver to you—Super Powers! Word!

P.P.P.S. Ok, for now I'm sure you've heard enough childhood stories. If you've made it this far in the book, THANK YOU! Now it's time to fast forward and get into some of the real estate stuff!

CHAPTER 11

Popped Cherries and Female Mechanics

In early June of 1998 I started real estate school. By the end of July, I had my license!

Back then you only needed fifty-four hours of classroom time to be eligible for the state licensing exam. The class cost $275, and it included the book. The state test cost $75.

My class instructor was Buford Eddy, who is still involved in the real estate business in northwest Indiana. Buford was probably in his midforties at the time; it's funny how that seemed old then! And now I'm forty-four years old. Man, does time fly! Buford stood about six feet tall and weighed in around 225 pounds; he was a very solid, well-built dude. He had jet-black hair that appeared to be colored, and I'm pretty sure he used that spray can stuff that helped cover bald spots.

Poor Buford, I used to think. I swear we spent at least half of our classroom time listening to him answer questions from the most lame-brained specimens on earth!

I'd look around the room and think to myself, why does real estate attract so many half-wits and know-it-all morons?

Buford said two very profound things to the class, and I'd bet dollars to donuts that I'm the only one from the class that has any recollection! First he said, "Real estate is easy to get into, easy to get out of, and everything in between is optional!" Even then, when I didn't really know a damn thing about the business…I really took notice. He also said, "List to last in this business!" I built my business around the idea.

The last class finally rolled around. Thank God, I thought. The only thing on the agenda that day was the final exam.

As I turned mine in, Buford said, "Hey, Bart, why don't we grab a pizza and a couple beers after class to celebrate!" I certainly like pizza and enjoy beer on what could be considered an alcoholic's level, but as usual I was the first to finish the exam, and I wasn't about to stick around while the rest of these retards labored through the remainder of the test! I politely declined the invitation and raced home.

Stacey and I had just closed on our first home in June of '98. We weren't married yet, so I lived there alone and slept in the guest bedroom. Stace would come over every day after work, and we'd play house until 9:00 p.m., when she would drive back to her mom's house where she was living. We wanted to wait to live together until we got married. Our wedding date was set for August 22, 1998.

It was during the home-buying process that I made up my mind that I wanted to be a real estate agent. Our agent, Marti, was nice enough but was below mediocre as an agent. She talked us into accepting the seller's first counteroffer, and she even talked us out of getting a home inspection!

Luckily nothing was wrong with the house, and it served us well for the four years we lived there. Later, I realized that most agents are like Marti, mediocre at best, and without a real understanding of what serving the client actually means…and certainly with no understanding as to how to run a business.

After passing the state exam, which was ten times harder than what the class prepared me for by the way, I joined the very first company I inter-viewed with, Century 21 Estates in Valparaiso, Indiana. I didn't know at the time that most brokerage business models are the same: take anyone that can fog a mirror and hope some of them actually figure out how to sell some homes!

David Remijan was the managing broker and was assigned to train me as a new real estate agent. The training consisted of one meeting a week for one hour, for a total of three weeks. Some of the training was very intense! He said that when on a listing interview I should bend down and look to see the gallon size of the water heater and say, I see you have a fifty-gallon water heater. "People love stuff like that!" he coached. He also said that I should make it a habit of stopping by a FSBO's house every day for like ten days just to say hi and see if they have any questions!

Can you imagine the number of restraining orders I would have had if I'd followed that advice?

I still remember the feeling I had when a girl in her late twenties en-tered the office one day while I was on floor time. She told the receptionist that she wanted to list her house. The receptionist called back to the phone at my desk in the office that I shared with three other agents.

"Hey, Bart, there's a lady up here that just walked in and she wants to list her house!" she said excitedly. I immediately had dancing butterflies in my stomach. I ran to the front of the building and introduced myself. Her name was Susan. She had dirty blond hair, a slight build, and probably stood five foot four.

I noticed two things right off the bat:

1. She was wearing a navy-blue button-up shirt with "Susie" stitched on a patch above her left breast.
2. She smelled like she would burst into flames at any time! Reeked of gasoline!

I ushered Susie into the conference room. "I'll be right back!" I said nervously. I then bolted directly into the office of Dave Remijan, who was intently reading the newspaper.

Dave had crisp, silver-gray hair, tanned skin, and was probably in his late fifties at the time. He studied the paper stoically with black readers perched upon his nose. "Dave! I have a lady in the conference room wanting to list her house!" I said proudly. "Can you come in there with me and help with the contract?"

"No," Dave said abruptly. "What else do you want me to do—wipe your ass? Get in there and figure it out!" he said, returning to his newspaper. I couldn't believe it! I was flabbergasted, flustered, and now even more nervous!

I raced back into the conference room with a blank listing contract. It turned out Susie was getting a divorce, and the house was only in her name. She was a mechanic at a local garage, which explained why her name was emblazoned on her shirt as well as the pungent smell of gasoline and the grease-encrusted hands.

After listening intently to her story, I turned to the contract. I read over the main points: contract length, list price, and commission. As you know, these are the only points of concern with most home sellers.

The contract was signed. I escorted Susie to the door and raced back into Dave's office. "Dave, I got my first listing!"

He wrinkled his nose and muttered, "Popped yer cherry, Bart. Now go get the damn thing sold, or it doesn't mean shit!"

Dave perplexed and even frustrated me greatly at first. He was intimidating and grumpy most of the time, but as I got to know him I really started to enjoy his no-nonsense approach. He once told me, "Bart, if you aren't going through at least a thousand business cards a year…you may as well flush 'em down the toilet, then maybe if you're lucky someday the plumber will find them and give you a call!"

I also remember Dave saying, "It's just business, Bart, nothing personal." This was after I decided to join another company, and he decided along with the owner to keep my listings. There's more on that later in the book.

CHAPTER 12

Sixteen Listings for $395

n March of 1999, Dave Remijan organized a group of agents in the office to go see a Roger Butcher seminar being held in Merrillville, Indiana.

Merrillville is ten minutes from Valparaiso and forty-five minutes outside of downtown Chicago.

At the end of the two-hour presentation, Roger offered a collection of his real estate sales programs for $395. I was the only one in our group to buy it, and likely the person who could afford it the least, but I was excited and determined to make a go of this real estate thing.

One of the ideas in the program dealt with Absentee Owners. He suggested we check with the local assessor's office and look up property tax records. We were instructed to send a short handwritten note to the owners when we found an address for a tax bill that was different than the property address. The note would say, "I am working with a handful of buyers in [name of whichever town the property was in]. I'm writing to find out if you'd have interest in selling your property at 123 Banana Street. Please call me right away at 219-405-3768. Sincerely, Bart Vickrey."

The note was written on a three by eight-and-a-half-inch notecard that had a black and white picture of me in the corner with the headline: From the Desk of Bart Vickrey. Sounds corny, right? Well, it worked!

Over the course of the first nine weeks after the Roger Butcher seminar, I signed sixteen listings because of sending out the misleading letter! Granted, most of the listings turned out to be overpriced turds, but I didn't know any better!

The main point I learned at that moment, and that I still take advantage of today, is that I have to be willing to invest in my business and myself. I've spent over $100,000 in my career on coaching, books, seminars, products, conferences, audio CDs—the whole shooting match! I would estimate that my return on investment on the $100,000 is at least tenfold, so over $1 million!

Never stop learning and never stop investing in yourself and in your business. As the great Jim Rohn once told me, "Work hard on your job, and you'll make a living; work hard on yourself, and you'll make a fortune."

Another important note to point out is that Stacey and I actually did something with the Roger Butcher ideas and information that we bought. We spent many days and many hours in the Assessor's office rifling through property tax records long before everything was available online.

Ideas are easy. Implementation is hard. Implementation is the difference between Mediocre and Meteoric.

At the end of this book, I'm going to outline for you the exact steps necessary to take in order to bring an *extra million dollars* into your business in the next five years or less! However, the Eighteen-Step Process means absolutely nothing if not acted upon, if not implemented into your business!

You can also find a down-and-dirty, abbreviated version of the Eighteen Steps to a Million at www.RealEstateGoodLife.com. On the site you will also be able to access all of the marketing material, book reviews, book reports, checklists, tracking sheets, and systems mentioned in the book.

All of the extras and bonuses and everything I just mentioned above is FREE on the site. I just couldn't fit it all in the book. So go take a look when you have time.

CHAPTER 13

Going Full-Time

It all started with a closing I had with one of the area's top agents. Let's call her Fawn. Fawn considered herself the "Queen of Real Estate," and she was the top agent in my area at the time. Apparently I impressed her during the transaction and she recommended me to her Broker. I was working part-time in real estate and full-time at a local gym as a personal trainer. The Broker worked out at my gym and was being trained by the manager of the gym, Mike. One day, Mike pulls me into his office and says, "Harry Glitz asked me to have you call him. He says you're a real estate agent. I had no idea! Is that why you carry a pager? Dan and I (Dan was the owner of the gym) thought maybe you were a drug dealer!"

I worked at the gym as an independent contractor. I established a base of personal training clients and then split the fees fifty-fifty with the gym. I didn't really care for Dan or Mike, so I never felt the need to get too personal with either of them.

Anyway, I gave Harry a call, and he said he wanted to meet. I told him I'd like to bring my wife, Stacey, along. He said, "That'd be great, Bart, and I'll have my office manager there as well!"

The meeting took place in December of 1999. The four of us met, and they dazzled us with compliments and possibilities and gave us the grand office tour. There was one major problem with the whole idea, however; Harry said that all of his agents were full-time and not allowed to work other jobs.

We left the meeting and drove directly to my mother's insurance office less than a minute away at the County Seat Plaza. On the short car ride over, Stacey said, "How soon do you want to start working there?"

"Uh, I'd love to but I can't," I said, feeling a little dejected.

"Why not?" asked Stacey.

"You heard Harry. His agents have to be full-time," I reported.

"Yeah, I know. You're quitting the gym and going into real estate full-time!" Stacey said confidently.

My mother had our baby girl, Madison, at her office during our meeting. "Well, how did it go?" my mother asked.

"Went great! Stacey wants me to quit my job and work there full-time," I said in almost a tattletale fashion, looking for my mother to set Stacey straight.

"You should go for it!" she exclaimed. "Sometimes you just have to take a leap of faith." This wasn't exactly what I was expecting, but deep down it's exactly what I wanted to hear. The two most important women in my life believed in me. What a great feeling!

January 7, 2000, I informed Frank Pressel, the owner of Century 21 Estates that I was leaving to join another real estate firm. Frank was fifty-three or fifty-four years old at the time, stood about six feet tall, topped the scales at around thirty pounds overweight, and had a slight lisp and a soft-spoken manner.

Frank's office was twice as big as Dave's and was always a little bit messy. Dusty plaques adorned the walls, along with at least one too many wooden ducks…never did figure out if Frank was a duck hunter or just liked to collect duck decoys, although I wouldn't have understood it either way.

"Thanks for meeting with me, Frank," I said nervously.

"Not a problem, Bart. What's on your mind?" Frank lisped.

"I've finally made the decision to pursue real estate full-time, but I'm going to make a fresh start with a new company."

"Congratulations on your decision to make real estate your full-time job, but I'll be sorry to see you go!" said Frank.

I'm not sure if he meant that or not. I just think there was no way for Frank to tell if I had any real potential at that point. He wasn't around a whole lot and neither was I, because I also worked a full-time job. I closed maybe two deals in 1998 after getting my license in late July. After getting married in August and then going on a honeymoon, I didn't really start working the business until mid- to late September of 1999.

In the last three months of 1999, I closed a whopping $792,000 in sales on seven transactions. So, I wasn't setting the world on fire, but I had confidence that I would make it work. That confidence was backed by my Bride Stacey.

Up until that point, Frank's impression of me probably wasn't great. He stood from behind his desk and approached me in what was probably a gesture to show me out of his office. I stood and matched his stride toward his office door. He squared his shoulders and said, "Can I ask which company you are joining?"

"Sure," I said. Once I told him Frank's demeanor immediately changed. His body stiffened, his nostrils flared, and his pupils narrowed.

I didn't know it at the time, but Frank and the owner of the office I was going to, were rivals and hated each other. They had been partners back in the early eighties, but their styles clashed, and the partnership ended bitterly.

Frank extended his hand, looked directly into my eyes, and chirped, "You won't make it six months at that office!" I remember his handshake was limp and clammy. I thought it was the emotions of the moment, but later when I made a play to buy his company, Frank and I had three or four secret meetings, and his handshake was always like that of a dead fish!

Frank's words ran through me like a ghost story around a fire at Camp Crystal Lake. At first it was fear I felt…maybe Frank knew something I didn't! Was I making a mistake? It was the second emotion that stuck with me…anger. Nobody was going to tell me I couldn't or wouldn't make it. I'd seen enough half-wits and butter-heads roaming the office somehow doing enough to make a living to know that I was going to make it in the real estate sales business.

That statement was immediately burned into my memory and has been accessed to provide necessary motivation several times over the years. On January 10, 2000, my full-time foray into real estate began. The Century 21 office I moved to was the number-one sales office in Porter County at the time, and it was owned by a local legend. Harry stood six feet tall, lean, with spiked gray hair, and he was always impeccably dressed with a bronze tan regardless of the season.

I walked into Century 21 a full-time agent on Monday, January 10, 2000. On Tuesday, I went to my first office meeting, where I was introduced as the new agent. Right after the meeting, I hopped on the "Fun Bus" for the caravan. Back in the day, we used to actually tour new office listings together as a group. Harry took it up a notch compared to the other offices and rented a little bus for us to be chauffeured around on!

After our tour of the homes, I ambled into the office and made a beeline for the Queen's office. "Hi Fawn, I was hoping that maybe sometime soon I can buy you lunch and pick your brain about the business?" I offered excitedly.

Fawn looked at me with raised brows and snipped, "Well, Bart...I'm awfully busy, you know." All the while she peered down her pointy, arrogant nose with her chin tilted up as if balancing a "Buzz Off" sign on it. I scurried off a little dejected but still eager to take on my new role as a full-time professional.

My exchange with the Queen had also offered another inspirational arrow in my ever-expanding quiver of motivational *incidents*!

CHAPTER 14

First Deal Implosion, Stacey Quits

When Stacey and I got married she was making good money as a financial advisor for Ameriprise Financial. Her boss was a maniacal, self-centered bitch that got off on manipulating people. Stacey had started at the company as a receptionist, moving her way up and finally getting her Series 6, Series 63, and Series 7 licenses. She was working as a Para planner!

Her boss, Lonna, never did like me. She always told Stacey that she should find an older and really rich guy to marry. Even after we were engaged to be married, Lonna told Stacey she needed to dump me when she found out I was allergic to cats! "You can't marry someone that is allergic to cats. Men break your heart; a cat never will," she told Stacey.

It was getting to the point that Stacey would get knots in her stomach on Sunday nights. She was so upset that the following morning would start another work week with the tyrant. Now that she was married to me, Stacey got even worse treatment from Lonna. She had less control and certainly less influence on Stacey now, and that didn't sit well with the ole bat.

In October of 1998, two months after our wedding, Stacey's mother, Sandy, was diagnosed with breast cancer. She had a mastectomy followed by reconstructive surgery. Stacey was still going into work each day but was leaving at 3:00 p.m. to drive up to Northwestern Hospital in Chicago to be by Sandy's side. Once her mother was released from the hospital, Stacey began to care for her daily, bathing her, draining the surgical drains, making her meals. Lonna didn't like it! She told the receptionist, "The sooner Stacey realizes that her place is at this office and not as some caregiver the better off we'll all be. That's what nurses and doctors are for!" Well, by this time everyone in the office liked Stacey a whole lot better than Lonna. The receptionist told Stacey what Lonna had said. Stacey told me, and I was outraged!

"You really need to quit!" I said.

"But we really need the money," Stacey countered.

"It doesn't matter to me if we live in a shed somewhere, as long as we're happy," I offered seriously.

The following Monday, Stacey put in her two weeks notice. Lonna arrogantly rebutted, "Two weeks won't be necessary. You can leave now!" She added sarcastically, "Have a great life." Later it was reported to us that Lonna said, "That idiot will never be able to support her." One more gallon of fuel for my fire, I thought.

It wasn't but a couple of days later that I heard Stacey crying in our bedroom. She had gone to bed early, and I was doing some very important late night fantasy football research with our dial-up Internet connection.

I ran upstairs, "What's wrong, honey?"

"I think I'm pregnant," she whimpered.

"Oh my God! That's fantastic!" I yelled, pretending not to be scared shitless.

"No, it's not; this is horrible timing!" she said.

I comforted her the best I could and then stumbled back downstairs thinking, "This shit just got real!"

That was November of 1998. Madison Ann Vickrey was born August 5, 1999. Between then and my first closing at Century 21 in June of 2000, we scrambled to pay our bills. We redeemed the $29,000 that Stacey had in a retirement account, and we grew more anxious and stressed during the no-income months at the beginning of my full-time real estate career.

I didn't know what the hell I was doing, but I was doing it! Holding open houses, sitting floor time, calling FSBO's—I even remember just calling directly out of the phone book! I would say, "Hi, are you thinking about selling your home, or do you know someone that is?"

It is amazing that still to this day very little training exists at real estate companies for agents looking to follow a step-by-step plan for success.

Anyway, I started to get some things cooking but had no closings in January, none in February, none in March, April, or May! Finally, my first closing since venturing full-time was on the books for June 5, 2000. It was a pretty good sale at $310,000! My commission was going to be over $4,000! Good thing too, because we were running out of money fast! We had burned through all of our dough and were now making ends meet with credit cards!

As that $310,000 sale scheduled for June 5 approached I was getting excited. This was going to be the biggest single check I had ever received.

I remember getting the call from the buyer, John, on Thursday, June 1. "Hey Bart, it's John. I've got bad news for ya buddy," he said softly. "Oh, no. What is it?" I asked. Maybe someone died or was sick? Nope...worse. "I'm not going to be able to close on that house. I need to back out of the deal," John said.

"I'm sorry to hear that. Do you need more time?" I said dejectedly.

"No, buddy, it's just not in the cards. Bank said I can't get the loan."

"Well, I'm sorry to hear that. I know your wife and kids really loved that house," I said, feeling worse for me than him.

I got off the phone feeling sick to my stomach and not really knowing what to do. I staggered into my broker's office and shared the news. "It happens sometimes, Bart. Have John get you a rejection letter from the bank, and we'll send it over with the mutual release to the listing agent," he advised.

I called John back, and he acted a little put out about getting the rejection letter from the bank. I told him it'd be no problem and that I could call the bank for him and explain what we needed. I truly thought this deal was dead. So, why not button it up ASAP and move on?

"Well, I'm real busy, Bart. I'll try to call the bank later. I don't have the number on me right now," he said arrogantly.

I told Stacey the bad news and didn't sleep very well that night.

The next day I got a strange phone call from John's wife, Doreen. "Hey Bart, my sister's in town. I'd love to show her the house. Any chance you can get us in?" Doreen said. She sounded like her usual excited self.

Now that's weird, I thought. From the very beginning, John had acted a little nonchalant about the whole thing. They had a beautiful home on the lake in a nice neighborhood in Valparaiso, but Doreen wanted some acreage and a smaller school system. She had targeted Washington Township, which is directly east of the city limits of Valparaiso and still has a Valparaiso address but is in a different school district. When I had met with them to walk through their house and help determine a value, John and I stood out on the deck overlooking the lake. John told me then that he really didn't want to move and that mowing acres of grass is not as much fun as fishing on this lake. This conversation flashed immediately back into my head as Doreen was unknowingly asking to see the house whose purchase John was now trying to sabotage and derail.

"Uh, Doreen, John must not have told you…He was turned down for the loan. You can't buy the house," Doreen's chipper demeanor changed on the phone.

"Bart, I'll call you right back!" is all she said, and she hung up the phone.

About an hour later, I got a call from John. "Look Bart, I really need your help on this. I don't want this damn house. I can't afford it while I still own our current home." I tried to talk them into making a contingent on sale offer and then listing their home, but Doreen insisted that she didn't want the stress. She wanted to be able to take her time moving. I ran and told my broker Harry everything. "Get me the file. Let's get this guy on the phone and figure this out!" Harry said.

I ran back to my cubicle, retrieved the file, and was back in Harry's office before you can say "real estate problems!" Harry dialed up John on speakerphone and we went over scenarios. Without a legitimate bank rejection letter he could be considered in default of the contract. Our contracts at that time had a 15 percent of purchase price penalty clearly written under the paragraph titled "Default."

Harry went on to explain to John that we would do whatever he wanted us to do, but that he might want to talk it over with his wife and his attorney before making any decisions. "I'll call you back," he said.

Doreen called back about an hour later. "Bart, we are buying the house. I don't care what John told you. That's my house!" she said.

The closing ended up being delayed until June 6, but it closed. Doreen was happy as a clam. Ole John never said another word to me. He didn't even make eye contact at the closing table! For some reason, he was mad at me. WTH?

CHAPTER 15

Myrtle Beach, October 2000

I t was Friday the 13th, 2000. We were finally at the closing table. The buyers were utilizing an FHA loan that had taken a couple of weeks longer than the loan guy had estimated. Why is it that mortgage companies have so little accountability?

Anyway, there we were on Friday at 4:00 p.m. closing with some of my favorite clients, Dave and Linda DeRose. The closing moved along just fine until the end when we were waiting and waiting for final funding for the loan.

At about five thirty the title company closer came out with everyone's checks, and Dave and Linda ran out the door. They were supposed to leave by five to pick up their kids, and now they were running late.

On Saturday morning we boarded a plane for Myrtle Beach. It was our first real vacation since our honeymoon back in August of 1998. In tow was our fourteen-month-old daughter Madison and both moms! It doesn't sound like a dream vacation to most to bring both mother-in-laws along, but we were blessed in that they both got along famously, and Stacey and I loved them both.

We rented a three-bedroom, three-bath condo right on the Atlantic Ocean in Garden City, South Carolina. Whenever I tell the story I say Myrtle Beach, because most people haven't heard of Garden City.

Myrtle Beach is eight miles north of Garden City right up Route 17. The condo was on the second floor with a balcony right over the gorgeous sand that stretched out about fifty yards before ceding to the sparkling waters of the Atlantic Ocean. Just to the south about one hundred yards was the famous Garden City Beach Pier, which was formerly known as the Kingfisher Pier before it was completely destroyed by Hurricane Hugo in 1989.

The pier stretched seven hundred feet into the ocean and featured an open-air nightclub. We spent a couple of nights dancing with Madison in our arms at that bar.

On Monday morning I got a call from my broker, Harry Glitz. "Hey, Bart, you gotta minute?"

"Sure, Harry. What's up?" I could tell he was on speakerphone. I'd seen Harry make many calls on speakerphone. He'd have someone in the room with him when it was an important call. I'm not sure why. Maybe he wanted a witness.

"I'm here with Debbie and we have some important questions for you," he said.

"Uh, OK," I replied. This must be serious. I'm on speakerphone, and there's a witness!

"This is a very serious matter, Bart, so we need you to be completely honest with us," he said.

What the hell? Now I was getting a little dancy in the belly. This wasn't a good dancy, like magical butterflies on your wedding day, or the thrilling tummy tingles from a white-knuckle ride on the Raging Bull at Six Flags in Gurnee, Illinois. These were the twisted, acidy knots associated with impending doom.

"Sure, Harry, what is it? Did I do something wrong?" I cringed.

"That's what we intend to find out," he offered unreassuringly. "On Friday you had a closing for 422 Sable Road. The sellers were DeRose. Did you forge the seller's signature on the pest inspection?"

"No, not at all. Why I would I do that? Did someone say I did?" I offered nervously.

Suddenly my heart sank, and I began to sweat and feel a little sick to my stomach. Did I forge their names? I was beginning to question myself! What the hell are you thinking? You've never forged anyone's signature. What in the world is happening?

"Listen, Bart, this is a big deal. If you signed for the sellers, we need to know the truth right now." His tone was accusatory. He sounded like he didn't believe me. He was looking for a confession like a grizzled detective. What a guy, I thought. My own broker thinks I'm some kind pest inspection forging creep!

"Look guys, I have no idea who signed the pest inspection. I cannot say that I saw or remember seeing the sellers sign it, but I know with one-hundred-percent certainty that it wasn't me!" Now I was getting a little agitated. Here I was on vacation, already stressed because I was broke, and now my broker and office manager were not just asking me but accusing me of forging a document in order to accommodate a closing.

I know what you're thinking; why in the world were you on a vacation if you were so broke. Well, our credit was really good, so we had a couple of nice credit cards available for us to keep up our appearance as a young, successful couple on the rise!

After a few more minutes and a couple of more questions, they finally let me off the phone. I didn't want to upset Stace, so I didn't tell her about the crappy call. In fact, I don't think I told her until months after the trip.

On Tuesday morning we all went for a peaceful walk along the white sand beaches on the Atlantic Ocean. The sun was shining, the temperature was in the low seventies, and the breeze off the water was fresh. It was a great day to be alive. Then my Motorola flip phone rang. I unsheathed it from the waistband of my swim trunks, pulled out the slightly bent plastic antennae, and flipped it open saying, "Hello, this is Bart."

The caller was my client Stephen Thompson. Right before I left, Stephen's home had sold. We had it on the market for basically zero days, so the sale had Stephen and his wife in a panic. Mostly Stephen panicked; his wife was pretty calm about the situation overall. Stephen was a stay-at-home dad if that's any clue for you. And who calls themselves Stephen when Steve is much more fun?

Anyway, Stephen had been a pain in the ass basically from day one. We met in a very unconventional manner. I had a listing about eight houses to the north of Stephen's. The sellers were relocating to New York and wanted a quick sale. Their relocation company was covering the commission and all of the moving expenses, so they priced the home very affordably, actually at $9,900 less than I advised them to! The first night the home was on the market I dragged two different clients through it. The first was Dave and Linda DeRose. We had been looking for a house for them ever since we got an acceptable offer on their home on Sable Drive. Dave and Linda made an offer on the spot.

An hour later I brought another couple through the house, and they also made an offer. This was exciting, but it put me in the middle of three couples, and I represented each of them. Now I know a lot of people don't believe in representing both sides of a real estate sale, but I've always felt that I did it better than anyone. It was just a mind-set that I had. When I was with the seller I represented the seller. When I was with the buyer I represented the buyer.

I presented both offers to the seller. I called back both buyers and let them know that there was another offer on the table, and that I represented each one. Dave and Linda raised their offer to one hundred dollars above asking. Ames and Connie decided to bow out. They felt rushed and pressured to make a decision, and we had just starting looking in general.

I felt bad for Ames and Connie. I told them I would find the exact same floor plan in hopefully the exact same excellent condition! The next day I drove to the neighborhood and jotted down the addresses of all the two-stories. This neighborhood was developed by one builder. That builder had four floor plans, a ranch, a cape-cod, a bi-level, and a two-story. Back at my office I wrote letters to all of the two-story homeowners explaining my situation.

By the end of the week Stephen called me back. "Are you just fishing for listings?" he asked.

"No, I really have a buyer that wants the two-story floor plan in your neighborhood." The fact that my sign was right down the road from him and now had a pending rider on it probably added the needed layer of credibility to my story.

"OK, well my wife and I are thinking of selling in the spring but this opportunity sounds at least interesting enough to investigate. When can you come by?" he said.

It was about 6:00 p.m. when he called. "I can come right now if that works for you," I said excitedly.

"Well, I'm not sure about that. The house is a mess," he countered.

"Look I've seen it all. A little mess is no problem. I know what my clients are looking for, and I can see if your home is a match within five minutes of being there!"

"My wife is probably gonna kill me, but come on over—she's not home from work yet!" he exclaimed.

When I arrived, Stephen was feverishly cleaning the house. As I approached the front door I could hear the vacuum running. He opened the door out of breath, "Hey come on in, just tidying up a bit!" he said as he wound up the vacuum cord.

Not only did the house look great, it smelled great! Within minutes of touring the main floor I knew this was the house for Connie and Ames! As Stephen and I completed the tour of the finished basement, his wife came home. "Hello?" she beckoned from the top of the stairs. For the life of me I cannot remember her name right now, and I'm on too much of a writing roll to stop and look it up...so get over it!

"Hi honey, this is Bart. He's a Realater." (Don't you love when people mispronounce Realtor?) "Bart sold the house up the road and had another set of buyers that want our floor plan," he said.

"Uh, OK, but we're not moving till spring, Stephen. We talked about this." Even she called him Stephen!

"I know, but I thought it wouldn't hurt to at least see if Bart thought his clients would like our house," he explained.

Next thing you know I've got Connie and Ames at the house, and they love it! We negotiated a fair deal for both sides and began showing Stephen and his wife houses. We probably looked at twenty homes over the course of two days. We found a great house for them and got an accepted offer. It wasn't easy though. Stephen pestered the shit out of me from the second he signed the listing agreement, then through to getting an offer on his home, and then through to putting in an offer on the home they were buying. He was a nervous son of a bitch to say the least!

On the Wednesday before we left for Myrtle Beach Stephen got the radon results from his purchase. The measurement was 4.4 pCi/L (pico-Curies per liter, but you know what it stands for!), so it was 0.4 over what the EPA considers safe.

Stephen did what Stephen does best. He freaked out! I did what I do best; I calmed him down. We talked through it, and requested that the seller install a mitigation system. The seller and their agent thought it was ridiculous. They didn't even know what radon was. This was right before radon really took off as a consistent deal killer for us in the business!

It was all settled, and Stephen was again excited about his sale and purchase, or at least that's what I though while I was on vacation in sunny

Myrtle Beach. I know, I wasn't actually in Myrtle Beach, but nobody's heard of Garden City…so just let me tell the damn story, would ya? Lol!

So Stephen was on the phone, and he was hysterical! "We're not buying the house. We need to back out! You gotta get us out of this deal!" he yelled. .

"Why, what's up, what happened?" I tried to ask calmly.

"I've been talking to my father-in-law. He and I have been doing a lot of research on radon. It causes cancer! Did you know that? Why didn't you tell me radon causes cancer?" he quizzed.

"Stephen, I told you before, people are just starting to learn about in our business. We don't have any hard proof that it causes cancer under normal living conditions in the household. But what I do know is that the EPA says any radon gas in the air up to 4 picoCuries is considered safe," I retorted.

"Well, I don't like the feel of it! Doesn't seem safe to me. And I'm not risking my family's life over a house with radon! Tell the sellers the deal's off!"

I tried to explain that the mitigation system would have the levels under 1 pCi/Ls, but he had made up his mind. He wanted out of the deal!

Here I was on vacation with the four most important people in my life all of whom were walking in front of me as I trailed behind…on my damn cell phone trying to keep one lousy deal together! Because I had to keep the lousy deal together!

I then called the listing agent and explained the situation. He was pretty upset. His mood was different when he called back. Surprisingly the seller was kind of relieved to let this buyer out of the deal. He was having trouble finding a home to buy, and was still upset about the whole radon "hogwash" as he called it.

When I got Stephen back on the phone to give him the good news he didn't even thank me. All he was concerned with was how soon I would be back in town so they could start searching for the next house. I explained to him that I had people watching my business while I was out of town, and I could hook him up with them. They could start looking right away if he wanted. "Bart, we're comfortable with you, and you know what we're looking for. So we'll wait. But we'll need to start looking like the day you get back in town. Will you be back in the morning on the twentieth? Maybe you can have showings already set up for us?" he said, sounding both demanding and as if he was doing me a favor by waiting for me. And he kind of was, since I'd have to pay someone a referral fee for finding them a home without me!

"No, we won't be back until late on Friday, but I can have homes set up for Saturday." I offered.

"OK, I guess that will have to work," he said.

What a great start to a vacation! On Monday I'm accused of forgery, and on Tuesday a deal falls apart!

On Wednesday we had a great day at the beach. The weather was beautiful and we all laughed, talked, and watched Madison run in and out of ankle deep water with a smile plastered upon her face ear-to-ear.

We had an early dinner at The Original Benjamin's in Myrtle Beach, where we stuffed our faces full of all-you-can-eat crab legs. After dinner we browsed through a used bookstore. A used bookstore, Barnes and Noble's, and the library are to me what porn is to some guys!

I bought two books that night, one of which would completely change my life. The first was *How to Make Millions with Your Ideas* by Dan Kennedy. The book cost me two bucks and would not change my life. I wasn't sharp enough at the time to really grasp it, but Dan's ideas were incredible. Later, around 2011, Dan Kennedy would change my life with books like: *The Ultimate Sales Letter, The No BS Guide to Marketing*, and *The No BS Guide to Time Management*. The second book I bought had an interesting title that caught my eye, also from the two-dollar bin. It was called, *Think and Grow Rich* by Napoleon Hill.

Napoleon had been hired by Andrew Carnegie, a successful business-man and one of the richest guys in the world, to interview the most successful people in the United States and determine their secrets for success. The process took Napoleon over twenty years, and the resulting book was published in 1937. Although an old book, the contents (except for the weird chapter entitled "The Mystery of Sex Transmutation") are incredible and completely timeless. The book entered my life at the exact right time, and it has truly changed me forever!

Once I got my hands on that book, I devoured it over the course of the remaining vacation, and I still reread it every couple of years. If you'd like a free copy of the book, you can visit realestategoodlife.com and click on the Free Resources Tab.

The trip to South Carolina was great now that I look back on it. At the time, I was unable to truly enjoy it because of the stress that I allowed in my life. The call from my broker, the deal falling apart with my jackass client, and now the enlightenment provided by an incredible book—all these things had me thinking that there's got to be a better way!

I tell these stories to help paint the picture of what I went through until I finally started to "get it." I'm no rocket scientist, so it took me longer than it will take you! My hope is to try to eliminate some of the pain as you better your life and your business.

One last closing kick to the groin before I close this chapter. When I got back to town, I was all set to show Stephen and his wife six homes on Saturday. Of course, that meant working some more while on vacation to get them showings set up.

I called Stephen Saturday morning to confirm the showings. "Hey, Stephen, I'm checking in about our showings today. Do you want me to pick you guys up, or just meet you there?" Back in the day I liked having buyers in my car, because that's where you can really build rapport and deepen the relationship.

Now I don't show houses, but my team does all the time. It seems that rarely do they drive buyers around in their cars. It's not because they don't want to; the buyers don't want to. I think part of this is due to the fact that we are being thought of more and more as a commodity and not as a true professional and advisor. It's sad really.

"Bart, I'm glad you called. We're going to have to cancel," he said.

"Oh, OK, that's no problem. Is everything OK?"

"Well, it looks like we bought a house last night," he said hesitantly.

"Oh wow, tell me about it," I said as my stomach sank.

"My father-in-law is friends with a builder in Greenfield Creek, so we went and looked at his home over there, and he cut us a great deal," he explained. Greenfield Creek is the neighborhood they loved where the house they backed out of was located. The neighborhood was still under construction, about three-fourths of the way completed with a few homes still under construction.

WTF! I thought. "Why didn't you wait for me to get in town? I could have represented you for nothing. The builder would have paid my commission," I said.

"We wanted to do that, but the builder said we'd get a better deal without an agent," he countered.

What a bastard! Not only did I lose a nice sale that I had most certainly earned! But ole Stephen had negotiated a low listing commission because I had both sides of the deal and didn't really have to spend any time or money on marketing. Of course, with the idea that he and his wife were moving up to a more expensive home and using me as their agent, I stupidly agreed! Of course I was too dumb to put in a clause that increased the listing commission if they screwed me over on the buying side!

OK, I gotta move on in the book. Rehashing this story is starting to make my butt stink!

CHAPTER 16

Thanksgiving Snuff

On Thanksgiving of 2000, me, Stacey, and fifteen-month-old Madison were at Grandma Vickrey's for the holiday. Irene Vickrey, my dad's mother, was a saintly woman. She stood all of five feet tall and probably weighed in at all of ninety pounds. She had cropped silver hair, was always smiling, and had retained a hint of a Tennessee twang. Buck was six years older than fourteen-year-old Irene when he married her in the hills of Tennessee. They moved to northwest Indiana shortly after marrying, with Cookie, Irene's blind mother, in tow.

Buck had landed a coveted steel mill job at Andrew Carnegie's former steel plant, US Steel. Buck would work there until he retired in 1990. He would pass away from leukemia in 1997 at the age of eighty. My childhood had its uncertainties as you've read, but for as long as I can remember we spent every Easter, Thanksgiving, and Christmas Eve at Grandpa and Grandma Vickrey's house. After a great meal, football watching, and visiting with family, we started to discuss Christmas.

Each year we drew names to determine who we would buy a gift for. My brother said, "Don't put my name in the hat this year."

"Why not, honey?" questioned Grandma.

"Because I have to work on Christmas Eve. Me, Pam, and Brandon aren't going to make it this year," he said sadly.

My older brother Larry is a big family guy, and Christmas is by far his favorite holiday. I remember each year Larry couldn't wait to drag the tree out and start decorating it. He'd have a can of tree flock in each hand creating a huge flammable cloud around him as he worked. Remember that stuff? Christmas tree flocking spray…it smelled terrible, and I'm sure it was some sort of biohazard when inhaled. I wonder if they still sell that junk?

Anyway, it wasn't going to be the same without my brother on Christmas Eve. He and I always laugh and joke around like schoolboys under these circumstances, and I'm gonna miss him.

"Nobody should have to work on Christmas or Christmas Eve!" I chimed in. Everyone agreed.

Out of the side of her mouth, my sister-in-law Pam lets out a barbed remark. "Well, some of us have real jobs!"

The comment took me a bit off guard and knocked the wind out of me a little. I should have been used to those remarks from Pam by now, but it still hurt.

I've stored that comment in my long-term memory bank along with Frank Pressel telling me I wouldn't make it six months in the business and ole Fawn Rollins, the former Queen of Real Estate, arrogantly snubbing my lunch invite.

These incidents allow me to return for motivation whenever I desire. I'm not sure what it is about being a real estate agent, but we lack respect in the eyes of the general public. We're thought of as commodities and a necessary evil. If only people understood the hard work, dedication, and sometimes overwhelming stress that goes into it!

This is one of the several reasons I am writing this book for you, which is really for me. I've always had this recurring and persistent desire to hear, "You have completely changed my life! Thank you!" I can't explain the appetite for this yearning. I have yet to hear a single client in all my years utter such a phrase. So I continue to seek.

I have heard other things over the years…

There's been, "I'm tired of you always taking the buyer's side." This came after I had explained the home inspection that, according to the report and the building code, required hand railing on a deck elevated more than fourteen inches off the ground. Mind you, the seller was retiring from snowy northwest Indiana to sunny Arizona. We sold the house for full price in eight days. "I think you should pay for it, Bart. You certainly haven't earned all the goddamn money you are charging me!"

Why does our commission even come into the conversation? After all, didn't we already negotiate at the time of the listing?

I've heard, "If you can't show it to me now, I'll just call someone else that will!"

I've heard, "What's your commission? Really? My neighbor's son who works for the railroad and also has a real estate license said he'd charge me only four percent!"

Yes, I really did hear that, and the list can go on and on, as you know. You've heard some real doozies yourself, haven't you?

My goal in writing this book and in providing all the free resources, including marketing material, systems, and the blueprint for the Eighteen-Step Process to an extra million (all easily found at www.realestategoodlife. com)—the overwhelming and conclusive goal for me—is to hear from you, "Bart, you've completely changed my life!"

The point of the Thanksgiving story is simple. Do not hesitate or feel chagrined about using "I'll show you!" as a motivational force behind your drive and determination. God knows I've resorted to it on the multiple occasions throughout my career.

CHAPTER 17

Fake Boobs and White Boyfriends

They say life is stranger than fiction. Well, the interactions, conversations, and stories spawned in the real estate business are right up there with being stranger, and sometimes *much* stranger, than fiction!

In May of 2001 I got an offer on my listing at 182 North 175 West in Valparaiso. The house was listed at $239,900 and we eventually agreed on $230,000. One-and-a-half story, Tudor style, on just over an acre of land. The owners were Jim and Marsha Shabi (pronounced Shay-bee), whom I met while holding a new construction open house down in Kouts.

Jim and Marsha were both characters. Jim stood about six feet two inches tall with a frothy Fu Manchu mustache, a self-proclaimed Harley guy. You can picture him, since most all Harley guys dress and look alike. His surface was that of a curt, tough customer, but once you got past the facade he was a kind-hearted and very intelligent man.

Marsha was maybe five foot two with shoulder-length brown hair with random gray streaks. They were both the boss in the relationship, which made for interesting meetings with them. "Right, Bart? Don't you agree, Bart?" Whenever they'd disagree on something each would then try dragging me to their side.

The tentative closing date was June 15. By June 1, I was getting concerned. The mortgage company was not providing any confidence with their noncommittal and vague responses to my numerous inquiries.

The selling agent was turning out to be a lame duck as well. He was difficult to get a hold of and never had any answers to my questions. I called him up. "Hey Mike, it's Bart Vickrey. How's it going?"

"Good, I guess," he said. "Have you talked to the mortgage company lately?"

"No, I figure no news is good news, right?" he said, like the idiot he truly was.

"I talked to them earlier today. I can't get a real commitment out of them. Maybe you and the buyer can help me turn up the pressure a little bit," I said.

"Uh, sometimes I think it works against us when we bug them too much," he countered.

"Well, we're less than two weeks from closing with nothing confirmed. I'm getting nervous," I added.

"I'm sure we'll be fine, Bart," he replied.

June 10 rolled around, and I still hadn't heard anything. The mortgage company was telling me the file was in underwriting. Mike, it turned out, was a part-time agent with a full-time job. He was no help to me. By this time Jim and Marsha were calling me daily, their frustration levels becoming more apparent with each phone call. The house was all packed up except for essentials.

"Hi, it's Bart Vickrey again. I need to set the time for closing. We're only two days away."

"Well Bart the file is still in underwriting with a couple of conditions pending, and we're waiting on one final document from the buyer," Nancy said. Nancy is an underwriter for the company and was handling this particular file. Through a number of phone calls and rapport building, I now had a direct line to Nancy. We had established a cordial relationship.

The originator never seemed to have any answers for me, and Mike didn't provide any evidence to suggest that he gave a rat's can one way or another.

"We should probably postpone the closing a week or so to be safe," Nancy suggested. Oh great, I thought, the Shabis are going to kill me!

"Hey, Jim, it's Bart. Looks like we're going to push the closing till the end of the month," I offered. "What the fuck? I knew it! This closing probably won't ever happen!" Jim yelled. Jim always erred on the side of half-empty. "She probably can't get the goddam loan! What's a girl like her buying a house like this anyway?" Jim questioned.

Erika was black, single, midtwenties, and smoking hot! She had a bodacious body and artistically enhanced bazoombas. I'm not sure if Jim was being racist, sexist, or ageist (is that a word?). Any time a white person says something inquisitive, inflammatory, or otherwise, and the other party is black, it seems the go-to reaction is "that's racist!" And a lot of times it probably is but definitely not all the times. Anyway, I could write an entire book on the subject, and how I'm saddened that after all of these years we still can't all just get along.

"Jim, hang in there, I'm as frustrated as you. I just don't have to actually live through it as you are. So believe me when I tell you, I'm on top of it!" I reassured him.

"I know, Bart, but Marsha's nagging the shit out of me! The only person I have to nag is you!" he half joked.

As the end of the month neared, we were still unable to get straight answers from the mortgage company, and Mike continued on as the part-time agent. "We should know something any day now, Bart." Nancy reported.

The end of June came and went. Nancy suddenly stopped taking my calls, and Mike could not be reached. As a last resort I called Mike's managing broker and reported the timeline of events. "Let me get to the bottom of this and get back to you, Bart. This doesn't sound like Mike," he said.

Doesn't sound like Mike? What sounds like Mike? I can never get him on the phone to determine what Mike "sounds like!" I thought to myself.

Mike called back an hour later, "You trying to get me in trouble with my broker?"

"No, Mike, I'm trying to get this deal closed. You never call me back!" I responded.

"Let me call the mortgage company and get the closing date set," Mike said.

I didn't hear back from Mike until the following day. "The loan had been rejected," Mike said softly.

"Oh no! Why?" I cried.

"They gave me no details. Just said they couldn't pull it off," Mike replied.

I could feel the asphalt tearing my road-rashed skin right off the bones as Jim dragged my bound and gagged carcass angrily behind his Harley soft tail.

"There may be light at the end of the tunnel," Mike offered. Hope it's not a train, I thought. "Erika said she's already found another mortgage company. She really wants the house!"

"Let me talk to the sellers and see what they'd like to do. In the meantime, a rock solid commitment letter from the new lender would be helpful," I replied.

I called Jim and said, "Well, I got good news and bad news, Jim."

"Let me guess: she can't get a loan, but you're going to buy the house instead, so I don't kill ya!" Jim said sarcastically.

"The lender couldn't get it done. But Erika has already found a lender that says they can do it. She really wants the house," I said.

"Great, then she should have to pay more for it for making us wait so long!" he yelled. "I don't know, Bart. Let me talk to Marsha and get back to you. We may just take it off the market. This is all getting to be bullshit!"

Dammit! I really needed this closing! I worried that I would lose the listing, and to add insult to injury I didn't hear back from Jim until after the Fourth of July.

"Listen Bart, we'll continue with this buyer. We don't want to put up with all the horseshit showings again, but if it doesn't go through this time we're taking the house off the market."

"Sounds fair," I said.

"I will tell you this, Bart, Marsha and I have learned a lot living out of boxes the past few weeks. We don't need half the shit we have! We haven't even missed it!" he added.

"You're right, Jim—we all have way too much stuff cluttering up our lives!"

The projected closing date was August 20. Then August 31. Then September 10. September 30. October 12. October 19, and then October 26. The closing was scheduled for 3:00 p.m. We got the clear to close at 11:00 a.m.

"Jim, I'm calling to confirm the three o'clock closing. I just got off the phone with the mortgage company," I said, only half believing it myself.

"Are you fucking kidding me? Is this one of those episodes of *Punk'd* where you're totally bullshitting me?" Jim said enthusiastically.

"Hard to believe isn't it? Thanks for hanging in there with me, Jim," I offered. "I'll believe it when I'm walking outta there with a check! We'll see you at three!" Jim laughed.

The approved HUD-1 came by fax at around eleven forty-five. It looked pretty normal until I noticed the big fat elephant sitting right in the middle of the buyer's side of the statement. Loan origination: $10,250! Now, I knew I was relatively new to real estate, but this seemed outlandish!

Nervously I called Mike to make sure he got a copy and saw the huge fee demanded of his client. Shit! Of course no answer! The call went to voicemail: "Mike, it's Bart, just wanted to make sure you got the HUD-1. I'm not sure if it's a typo, but check out Erika's loan origination fee…it's over ten grand!"

I never did hear back from Mike before closing. In fact, he didn't even show up for the closing. Some other dopey agent showed up saying Mike had to work.

The Shabis showed up half an hour early. "We were too nervous to sit at home any longer!" Jim said.

I asked Mary Jane if it was OK for the Shabis to go on into the closing room early. "Sure Bart, send 'em on in. I'm still waiting on the closing package from the mortgage company anyway," she said.

WTH! The disappointments never ceased on this deal! Mary Jane was the in-house closing agent who worked for Ticor Title, but she had her office inside the Century 21 building. I liked Mary Jane. She was hardworking, knew her stuff, and always treated me a little better than the other agents, probably because I always treated her like gold.

At three o'clock the dopey substitute agent showed up as Mike's replacement. "Where's the buyer?" she dopily asked.

"Uh, I have no idea. You haven't talked to her?"

"No, I'll call her now," she stumbled as she fumbled through the file in her hands desperately searching for Erika's number.

At 3:05 Morris Day from the eighties group The Time showed up! If you're unfamiliar with Mr. Day, just Google him; you'll get a kick out of it. Morris was the flamboyant and charismatic lead singer of the The Time. They had a big hit back in the 1980s called "Jungle Love." Great song!

So, this Morris Day lookalike strolled in with a purple suit and matching hat hilariously adorned with a black feather in it! I'm not pulling your leg. Stuff like this cannot be fabricated! It turned out he was the mortgage guy! Holy shit! I had thought I was nervous even before I saw that this was the guy we had to rely on to make sure the loan would go through! Jim and Marsha just stared in disbelief.

"Erika's on her way," Morris said. (I cannot for the life of me remember his name.) "She's running a little late coming from her apartment in Chicago. Should be here any minute," he added.

At three thirty Erika rolled in wearing a skin tight, super short dress showing enough cleavage to hide a head of cabbage in. With her was a forty-something white guy with tanned skin and slicked back, jet-black hair.

"Sorry I'm late," she offered.

"Hi, I'm Bart Vickrey, and this is Jim and Marsha Shabi, the sellers." I introduced everyone.

"Oh, I know them," she smiled. "We talked during the home inspection."

She then stuck her hand out to the dopey agent sitting on her side of the table, "Hi, I'm Erika."

"Nice to meet you. I'm Valerie, your agent," said the dopey agent.

"Oh, hi…" Erika said sounding confused. "Have we met? I thought my agent was a guy?"

My God, I thought! This cannot get any better!

Mary Jane rushed into the room at about 3:40. "We have the package!" she said. "I'll need your IDs, and Erika I'll also need your cashier's check. And Bart, you probably have earnest money for me," she instructed. I pushed the earnest money check down the table. Jim looked it over as he continued its push down to Mary Jane.

Erika looked a little confused. She was rifling through the file she brought with her and was now rummaging desperately through her purse. In front of her she had already produced two cashier's checks but was still nervously pursuing something more. She then stopped, shrugged her shoulders, and whispered into her "attorney's" ear. I put attorney in quotes because Erika introduced him as her attorney when they arrived, but the vibe was completely different, so I wasn't buying it. More like Sugar Daddy!

"Uh, ma'am?" Erika whispered.

"Yes," said Mary Jane.

"I forgot my cashier's check at home. I got the one from my momma and my Auntie, but not mine. Can I mail it to you after the closing?"

"Uh, well…no we're going to need the check in order to close today," Mary Jane replied.

Jim Shabi looked over at me with eyes full of potential murder!

"Can I call my momma and have her bring it?"

"You sure can!" Mary Jane said as she pointed to the telephone in the corner of the room sitting proudly atop a small brown table.

Erika leaped from her chair grabbed up the phone and started dialing furiously. "Momma I need a favor. I forgot the check I need to buy this house! I don't know. No. I don't know; I just forgot it. I need you to grab it for me. I can't, I'm already here at the closing. I need it now or I can't buy this house. C'mon Momma, please. It's in Valparaiso, past Merrillville. I'll give you the address. Why not? Please! All right, I'll meet you at Indianapolis Boulevard at the Shell station. OK, thanks Momma. Please leave now, OK?" Erika hung up the phone.

We all stared at her. "I'm-a meet my momma at the border to pick up the check," she said, meaning the state border between Indiana and Illinois.

"She can't bring it all the way, huh?" Mary Jane quizzed.

"No, she say she too busy," Erika replied.

She then gathered her huge purse and her man friend and was off. "I'll be right back," she added.

I turned to Jim and Marsha, "Why don't you guys go home and relax? I'll call you as soon as she gets back. She has a lot more papers to sign than you guys anyway. She can get a little head start when she returns, and you won't be stuck here the whole time," I offered.

"This isn't going to close today, is it?" Jim exasperated.

"If she comes back, we should be fine," I said half joking.

"Well, we're not going anywhere. We'll just stay here, and hopefully she comes back. But if we don't close today, this goddam deal's off! My heart can't take too much more of this shit!" Jim's voice steadily raised as he talked.

I got up and walked into Mary Jane's office, which was attached to the closing room.

"Oh my God, Bart, do you think she's even coming back?" Mary Jane whispered.

"Well, I sure hope so. I'd hate to think this is some sort of sick joke or something!" I replied.

I staggered back into the closing room and offered to get Jim and Marsha a beverage. Jim wanted coffee and Marsha a Diet Pepsi. As I left to retrieve the drinks, Morris Day followed me out. "Mr. Vickrey, here are some business cards. I hope I've earned some future business by getting this one to go through for you," he said proudly.

If this one goes through, I thought to myself. I accepted the cards and studied them with feigned interest. "Why has the file been so tough?" I asked.

"The buyer makes very good money but cannot show any proof. There's no paper trail. She also has a lot of credit card debt and a nine-hundred-dollar car payment," he offered.

"Nine hundred dollars?" I asked.
"Yes. She drives a beautiful new Jaguar."

At this point I found myself wondering what nationality this guy was. He looked black, dressed black, but now I noticed he had some sort of accent. Indian maybe? A Saudi? Oh, who really cares? I thought. Let's just get this hell ride over with!

I called Stacey from my office. "I'm going to be late!"

"Oh no, why?" she quizzed.

"If I told you now you wouldn't believe me, so I'll save it with hopes this thing actually closes! I will say this. The story includes a ten-thousand-dollar origination fee, a loan officer in a purple suit driving a purple Mercedes that looks just like Morris Day, there's fake boobies, and a Sugar Daddy!"

"Oh my God, how crazy. I can't wait to hear it! What time do you think you'll be home?" she asked.

"Not really sure. But you should just plan on going without me. I'll meet you there, so you don't have to be waiting around for me," I said.

We had plans to go to a Halloween party my brother was hosting. Stacey would be Cleopatra and I Marc Anthony. Little Madison would be a bumblebee.

Stacey hates to be late to anything, so I knew that giving her the clear to leave whenever would prevent a little stress for her and would save me multiple nagging phone calls.

"OK honey. Me and Mads will meet you there. Please hurry. I'll miss you!" she said.

Erika and Tan Man the Sugar Daddy returned at quarter past five. That wasn't too bad, I thought, considering it takes a good thirty to thirty-five minutes to get to the state line from Valpo.

Mary Jane collected all three cashier's checks. I'm not sure how that was working. I guess Erika's mom and aunt were gifting her money to buy the house. Whatever works, I thought. She then passed out the HUD-1 for all to review. Immediately, Tan Man Attorney looked up at me with a frown and without saying a word pointed to the ten thousand dollar origination fee!

Oh no, time for the deal to die, I thought. I just shrugged and pointed to Morris Day. Tan then turned to Erika, pointed, and whispered in her ear. "Yeah, I know about it," she told him. Whew, she knew about it, cool, let's continue.

We went through the docs for both sides. Signatures and idle small talk. Jim wasn't saying a word, but Marsha and Erika were discussing the house. We were just about done with signatures. Mary Jane was at the head of the table shuffling papers. And Erika said, "Oh yeah, I almost forgot." She then reached in her duffle bag sized purse, pulled out a wad of cash, and handed it to Morris Day! What the fuck is going on here! My confused brain yelled to me.

The cash was in a roll with a rubber band, exactly how a drug dealer would carry it around. It was probably about an inch in diameter and the exterior bill was definitely a Benjamin. This is going down in history, I thought excitedly to myself.

Tan Man looked as shocked as the rest of us. He quickly caught my stunned eye and raised his eyebrows in horror and disbelief. He then leaned over and whispered again in Erika's ear. "Don't worry about it," she said. "It's what we agreed to." Morris happily accepted the wad of dough and stuffed it inside his suit coat.

I quickly caught sight of Mary Jane out of the corner of my eye and turned to find her with mouth agape in utter disbelief! She quickly grabbed all the papers, stuffed them into a folder, and said, "I need to get funding. Will we get funding after hours on a Friday?" She looked at Morris.

"Yes, ma'am. They should be on standby for ya!" Morris said proudly.

Mary Jane disappeared into her private office. About fifteen minutes later she reappeared. "They want to speak with you," she instructed Morris.

Oh shit! Here we go, there's no way this made-for-TV movie of a deal can possibly go through, right? This is where it ends! Morris is going to come running back out of Mary Jane's office and yell April Fucking Fool's or something like that…isn't he? The little voice in my head was going nuts!

About ten minutes later, I excused myself and staggered back to Mary Jane's office. Her office was kind of a makeshift, afterthought type of a set up. It appeared that it had originally been part of the closing office, and somebody just threw up a wall, added a door and another wall…and said here's your office. Although she did have two workstations, one for her and one for her assistant. Mary Jane was seated in her spot, while Morris was on the phone in the other.

"How we lookin'?" I quizzed.

"Not good, Bart. We still don't have a funding number," Mary Jane replied. "He's on the phone with the home office trying to get it worked out."

It was now six thirty and this son of a bitch closing had started at three, or was at least supposed to start at three!

Back in the closing room, Erika and Marsha were discussing Erika's landscaping plans, Jim had his big meat hands clasped behind his head and was staring at the ceiling, and Tan Man was faking interest in the landscaping conversation. Valerie, the dopey stand-in agent for Mike, was long gone. She had left about an hour ago asking me to call her when the closing ended. Yeah right!

At quarter to seven both Morris and Mary Jane stumbled out of the back room.

She looked directly at me with a can-you-believe-this look in her eyes and said, "We're all good. Congratulations." She then passed out copies of documents to appropriate parties, and checks to me, the Shabis, and to Morris. We all stood, shook hands, and I ushered everyone out of the closing room toward the open staircase leading to the main floor. We walked past the reception area, and I held open the glass doors that led to another set of glass doors, which then led to the parking lot.

Jim and Marsha thanked me profusely with big-toothed grins. "Let me know when you want to grab some beers and celebrate," Jim said.

"Sounds great guys. That'd be great!"

Finally at seven o'clock, the four-hour, five-and-a-half month closing was done.

Exhausted, I made my way around the reception area, which opened on either side to the staircases, one up, one down. It was a contemporary building, and the staircase was made out of steel, not exactly floating, but the treads were suspended with diagonal uprights and no visible risers, so you could see right through them.

In front of the stairs was a little nook area that housed the copier. Mary Jane stood next to it staring at what appeared to be a check, probably making more copies of things from the closing we just finished.

As I headed up the stairs to dash into my office and grab a few things before heading out to the Halloween party, Mary Jane said, "Hey Bart, you're not going to believe this…I think Erika's cashier's check is a phony!"

Real Time Update:

I wrote this chapter while on a plane from Chicago to Orange County, California. The date was July 22, 2015.

We stayed in Anaheim and spent the first three days at VidCon, an insane conference for people that use video in their life or business that has mainly turned into a place for YouTubers to be treated like rock stars. Did you know that there are dozens of people that now make over a million bucks a year posting videos on YouTube! It's crazy!

My middle child Maya is really into YouTube and YouTubers. She'd been talking about VidCon for the past few years, so we decided to take the kids and make a vacation out of it. You can see a little video I put together of our time there, just visit YouTube and search Bart Family at VidCon.

After the conference ended, we hired a driver to take us to downtown LA, the Hollywood sign, Beverly Hills, Rodeo Drive, and the Walk of Fame at Hollywood Boulevard. Seeing downtown LA is insane. There is the beautiful Staples Center where the Lakers and Clippers play, a clean and crisp couple of blocks where the government buildings are, the financial district with the high-rises, and then it's a wasteland. The clean and chic cityscape becomes blocks and blocks of homeless people clamoring around like the walking dead, with tents lined up one after the other. It was very sad to see that many broken people in one place. I'm not sure what the solution is, but I'm sure we can do better than that!

Rodeo Drive was exactly as we expected: really cool stores, tons of fancy cars tooling around, and a bunch of well-dressed, beautiful people.

The Hollywood sign was awesome and so was driving through the Hollywood Hills to get there. Hollywood Boulevard on the other hand was a huge disappointment! If I never visited again, I'd be just fine. The place was packed and mixed in with the crowd were a lot of creeps, and a bunch of pushy peddlers trying to sell bus tours.

We ate lunch at the Rusty Mullet, kind of a cool dive bar. The walls inside were decorated with murals of a whole family of mullet-wearing hillbillies. Leather booths lined the walls, and the windows opened out to provide a really cool open air feel that put you right in the action of the psychopaths, derelicts, Chinese tourists, fake Elvises and tour bus peddlers.

While we were in the Mullet, a shirtless guy with tanned, leathery skin in his midsixties crossed the intersection wearing shiny, tight booty shorts and a bedazzled hat that said SEXY. He strutted through the intersection flexing his sagging biceps! What a display!

The following day we walked over to Disneyland. We figure we'd outsmart the crowd and go there on a Monday. Wrong! The place was wall-to-wall Mickey worshiping revelers! Our spoiled kids have been to Disney multiple times, but we've always gone to Disney World, so it was nice to visit the original.

During our stay we ate at P.F. Chang's twice, Cheesecake Factory twice, Bubba Gump Shrimp, and Tony Roma's. We stayed at the Desert Palm Hotel right around the corner from the entrance to Disneyland.

Next door to the hotel was a 7-Eleven that we stopped in a couple of times at the end of the night. The first time in it was me, Madison, and Deuce. Stace and Maya continued on into the hotel. Madison grabbed a candy bar, Deuce a baby bottle candy (a sucker shaped like a baby bottle that is then dipped into a vat of flavored sugar), and I wanted a Miller Lite nightcap.

As I approached the coolers in the back, I saw a sign over the beer cooler: "Buy One Get One." I read the sign out loud with excitement as I opened the cooler door. Two coolers down a street bum was eyeballing his cooler's contents. He must've heard what I said because he shouted, "That's how you fuckin' do it!" I looked over and smiled. His eyes were dark and distant.

I turned on one heel and headed back up the candy aisle and nearly ran Madison over. I didn't realize that both kids had trailed directly behind me like a couple of baby chicks following Momma. Madison and I locked eyes, and we both gave the wide-eyed can-you-believe-that? look to each other.

We all lined up to pay when I noticed another bum at the Icee machine. The bum yanking on the Icee handle wasn't the oddest part. It was the large colorful parrot that was residing on the bum's right shoulder that left me speechless!

I turned back toward the cashier just in time to see the beer cooler bum swiftly exiting the store without a purchase. He had a large can of cold 7-Up sticking out of his back pocket! What the hell is going on around here? I thought excitedly to myself. I was a little scared to be honest.

We paid and hurried out toward the hotel. Directly in front of the 7-Eleven stood a covered bus stop where about eight bums were hanging out. As we scurried along the parking lot crossing into the hotel's property, I asked Madison, "Did you see that bum shoplift a can of pop?"

"Yes! And he's over there hanging out with those other bums at the bus stop!"

Back in the room, we told the story to Stacey and Maya. Our room was a corner-unit suite that had spectacular views of the 7-Eleven parking lot and the hobo bus stop. The windows in our room were large and opened by sliding from right to left.

We all gathered around the window and literally watched and listened in to a live bum reality show, which gave me a brilliant idea. BumLife.com! We would visit all the major bum-infested cities and follow bums around with a video camera and audio crew. We could hear their stories, talk to their multiple personalities, maybe even witness some bum romance, and probably even catch some live bum brawls! Talk about a great reality show!

We had a blast! Vacations are always the best for us as a family because it forces the kids to spend time with us!

I'll see you again at the next Real Time Update!

CHAPTER 18

Why I Hired My First Assistant

My office overlooked the parking lot at Century 21 Executive Group. It was after hours on a Friday night in the middle of December in 2002. I was the only person left in the building.

My cell phone rang. It was Tony Ramon. "Hey Bart, I need a huge favor," Tony slurred. "I had a huge fight with Maria and stormed outta the house, but I forgot my damn wallet! I was going to get a hotel room, but I don't have any cash on me. Can I sleep at your house tonight?"

Tony was a client of mine. He and his wife Maria were wannabe homebuilders. We had just closed on their very first spec home. I had both sides of the deal (nice)!

I had spent a lot of time with Tony during the long process of building a spec home. He called me a lot, picked my brain, asked tons of questions, and had me review dozens of floor plans. He finally bought a lot, decided on a floor plan, built the house, and I had it under contract within three weeks of listing it. I didn't consider Tony a friend, but apparently he felt different—given that now he was asking to sleep at my house.

"Sorry Tony, I'd love to help but Stacey and I have a four-month-old at home and little Madison is only three," I replied.

"I can sleep in your basement. Nobody will even know I'm there." He was pleading with me. "I'm just not comfortable with it, buddy," I said.

"Well, OK, could you lend me a few bucks so I can get a hotel room?" he said.

"Sure, let me see what I have," I said as I reached into my left front pocket.

"All I've got is forty bucks," I said staring at the crumpled twenties.

"You still at the office?" Tony quizzed.

How did he guess that? I thought to myself. "Yes, unfortunately I'm still here."

"I'm right up the road. See you in a few," he said.

Seconds later I saw headlights turn into the parking lot. Wow, he was right up the road! I thought feeling just a little creeped out. Was he already nearby and saw my car in the lot before he even called? Weird.

I made my way down the stairs from the second floor and unlocked the front door. The cold air immediately whipped in and reminded me how crappy it is to live in Valparaiso, Indiana, in the winter.

"Hey buddy! Thanks a million. You're a life saver," Tony remarked as I handed him the dough. As soon as his pie hole gaped I whiffed the sour scent of booze. "I'll pay you back as soon as I get my wallet," he said.

This was weird. And it was late. "You gotta get him outta here," said the voice in my head. I hurried the conversation, reminded Tony it was late and I needed to get home, and ushered him back out the door where he had stumbled in.

When I got back up to my office I looked out and to my befuddled amazement witnessed a small part of humanity die. As Tony approached his car he made a small zigzag to his left and stopped. He then unzipped his jeans and took a steamy leak right there in the now victimized parking lot.

What the hell is going on around here? I thought. It wasn't just about this moment, me witnessing the mournful end of civilized society as we know it, but, why in the world was I even at the office on a Friday night at 8:30 p.m.? Why? My poor wife was at home with our two babies, and I was here.

There's got to be a better way!

I immediately started making a list of everything that I did in my business, which, as I was a solo agent at that time, was everything!

I then organized the list by dollar value. What is it worth? What would it cost me to pay somebody else to do it? Most of the list fit into the eight to twelve dollars an hour category. The high dollar stuff like meeting with buyers and sellers, creating lead generation systems, and communicating with my database were only getting a fraction of my hours worked.

This had to change!

It was only my third full-time year in the real estate business, and I was literally working seven days a week.

Stacey called at 9:35 p.m. "Hi, honey. You coming home soon? I'm getting worried about you," she said. "I'm leaving now, and I have an idea." If I had a dollar for every time I said that to Stacey we'd be living on a tropical island right now.

Soon after this unforgettable night, I hired my first assistant. She started part-time because, of course, I didn't think I could afford her. My business doubled within the next twelve months. My time off time increased as well.

It's kind of sad the trick bag we create for ourselves as real estate agents. We work our butts off to provide for the people we love and cherish the most in life. In doing so, we create a business that requires us to spend most of our time away from the very people that we love and cherish most in life.

Treat your business like a business, and one day you'll have one! Word up!

CHAPTER 19

Christmas Party Gate Crasher

T he Sand Creek Country Club is located in Chesterton Indiana no more than ten minutes from the shores of Lake Michigan. It is now the epicenter of the exclusive gated neighborhood Sand Creek and is surrounded by an award-winning, championship golf course.

In 1969 the Bethlehem Steel Corporation fired up the blast furnace at its new steel plant located in Burns Harbor, Indiana. The new plant now, along with other mills in the region like US Steel, made northwest Indiana the most productive and efficient steel-making region in the world!

Along with the lakefront purchase in Burns Harbor, Bethlehem Corporation bought thousands of additional acres of land in and around Chesterton.

In 1974, six-hundred acres was allocated for the development and construction of Sand Creek. The master plan included an eighteen-hole golf course, tennis courts, swimming pools, and the main clubhouse, which included a bowling alley.

In the early eighties the economy was in a full recession. By 1983 the club was opened to the general public, and in 1985 Bethlehem sold the club to North American Equities.

In 1991, the Lake Erie Land Corporation took over, and in 1997 the magnificent, brand-new, 55,000-square-foot two-story clubhouse was unveiled.

This incredible retreat for rich people sits proudly atop an elevated bluff. The surrounding grounds are meticulously landscaped with local indigenous plants, flowers, and bushes. As you saunter your way up the sweeping walkway toward the grand entrance, you are escorted by flowering orchids, billowing dune grass, sweeping views of fully mortgaged McMansions, and beautiful winding fairways.

I remember my first golf outing at Sand Creek. My jaw unhinged and nearly struck the floor upon entering the men's locker room. Inside were high ceilings, dark wood paneling, plush carpeting, and a full service fully stocked bar with a well-dressed bartender at the ready! The lounge area was accentuated by plush leather overstuffed chairs and three large flat screen televisions. Damn! Rich people problems, right?

Well, to get to the point: the Grand Ballroom located within the plush Sand Creek Country Club would be the home of the 2003 Christmas party. And I couldn't wait!

I'm kind of a strange bird, but you've probably already figured that out. I mean c'mon, who in their right mind goes into the real estate sales business and doesn't like to make phone calls? That would be me! I currently make no phone calls in my business, and I built my entire career on next to no cold calls.

Who'd rather sit in his basement and watch football on television and turn down tickets to go watch the game live in person? Still me.

Every year someone invites me to Chicago to see to see the Bears feebly battle the Green Bay Packers. I'm a lifelong cheese head named after world-class quarterback Bart Starr and one of the greatest coaches to ever live, Vince Lombardi (my middle name is Vincent).

I've been to Bears games before. Their fans are brutal. Why would I subject myself to such buffoonery or risk getting stale beer splashed onto my vintage 1967 Bart Starr jersey? Ain't gonna happen! You'll find me in my climate-controlled basement surrounded by other civilized Packer Backers!

Another anomaly is that I'd rather be in the corner reading a book than socializing with a group of people. However, once properly enticed to attend a party…yer gonna have to drag me out kicking, screaming, and likely inebriated!

Which brings us to my giddy anticipation of the company Christmas party. My favorite party style format is the wedding reception. Nice meal, great reason to celebrate, open bar, and dancing. I've always liked dancing.

When I was three years old, I'd jam the Merle Haggard eight-track into the tape deck and gyrate and shimmy to the beat. I'm not sure why I always chose ole Merle. Maybe it was the only tape we had? And I really don't have any recollection of that story, but my ninety-four-year-old granny tells it at least once a year! Apparently I played the tape so much it broke!

I do fondly remember loading up the Gap Band V cassette into the Pioneer stereo housed in the corner of our dining room. The kickass hi-fi was one of the few possessions that mom's second husband, John, brought into the marriage. I got a ton of ear-blasting fun out of that stereo!

End of tangent. Back to story.

Leading up to the Christmas party, there had been some salacious rumors about the Broker having a torrid love affair with secretary of the top agent in the office. If smoke does indeed indicate fire, then five alarms would apply here. (Wow! Sometimes poetic stuff just comes out of me!).

The party night arrived and people were dressed up and sporting their significant others. The Broker had gone all out! Full-service open bar, live band, and a wonderful dinner. We were served a beautiful filet and delectable salmon.

As you know, real estate agents like to drink and sometimes get wild. This night was no exception. Liquor was flowing, music blaring, and it was fun for all!

There was tension in the air from the beginning of the night. The rumors of the Broker and office assistant had been at a fever pitch leading up to the party. There was even a rumor that the agent whose alleged floozy secretary was having the affair had confronted him about it, and he denied everything.

During the evening I noticed that separately both the assistant's husband and the Broker's wife were getting loaded. Another clue that the situation might be coming to a head. I'd been around his wife in several social settings prior to this night, and I don't think I'd ever seen her drink more than one glass of wine in an evening. On this night she was drinking like a sailor.

She did say something hilarious to me that night that I've been using ever since. "You look lovely as always," I told her.

"Thanks Bart, not so bad yourself."

"I love that Gerry wore a tux. He looks sharp!" I added, pointing at Gerry across the room. "Phhffftt…he's good from afar but far from good!" she slurred.

So the night rolled on, and I looked over from the middle of the dance floor into the crowd of onlookers. You know how in a party situation like this there are the dancers, those congregated around the bar, the early leavers, and then the dance floor onlookers. The onlookers secretly wish they had the guts to be dancing, but they typically sit with other onlookers making fun of the dancers!

Anyway, in the crowd I saw the assistant to another top agent in the office, sitting on the alleged adulteress's husband's lap just jabbering away about something. It turned out she was providing candid details about the alleged affair between the two. Next thing you know there's an exchange of words near the bar between the Broker and the husband followed by a screaming match with said adulteress and her husband in the hallway just outside the ballroom.

No more than ten minutes later I saw the metal shutter to the bar closing, and the band abruptly silenced their instruments. It was ten minutes after eleven, and the party was scheduled to end at midnight.

"What's going on?" I asked.

"I think everyone's probably had enough, so I'm shutting it down," he said calmly.

The assistant was in the hallway sobbing, some of the ladies had her surrounded and were consoling her. As we all started to make our way out of the ballroom I heard, "Bart, carry me!" It was Gerry's wife smiling from ear to ear and drunk as a skunk! I flung my arm around her waist for stability, and she reached up and nearly had me in a half nelson choke hold.

Once we made it to the front door, Gerry and his son-in-law took over the escort. Stacey and I walked in the crisp air to our car and drove the winding road out of the Sand Creek neighborhood. As we approached the gate and guardhouse, I noticed two odd things.

First, the gate was open only three quarters of the way, and it appeared to be crumpled right at the big S emblem, with a handful of the vertical iron bars twisted up like a pretzel.

Second, there were clear tire tracks rutted into the grass to the right of the gate-blocked road.

"Hmm, that's not good," I whispered to my slack-eyed Bride.

Back in the office on Monday the story spread like a California brush fire! Some of it was accurate, some wasn't.

- The two guys brawled in the parking lot. Not true.
- The husband drunkenly plowed his minivan into the elaborate, custom-built, beautiful Sand Creek iron gate. Unfortunately 100 percent true.

- The Broker signed a check for $15,000 to replace the grotesquely damaged gate. Sadly true.
- The accused left their spouses to run off together. Not true.
- The last ever wildly over-the-top Christmas party at Sand Creek or any other country club happened that night. Dammit, that one's true.
- The assistant and husband immediately sold their home and moved out of town due to public shame. Not sure the reason, but they did leave town.
- The Broker eventually divorced due to another alleged affair. Unfortunately true.

Ahh, the good ole days. It's fun to reminisce and share these old stories!

CHAPTER 20

Left for Re/Max

O n Saturday, February 14, 2004, I packed up my office and waited nervously for his arrival.

His BMW turned into the parking lot about 10:00 a.m. I gave him a few minutes to get settled in before I made my approach.

One of the many things that I did admire about Gerry was that he came to work every day and often on Saturdays. He'd usually arrive around nine thirty or ten on Saturday and be outta there no later than one in the afternoon. Weekdays he'd typically arrive by eight thirty and would stay till six or six thirty.

I remember him telling me in my first year, "Sorry about that, Bart. I'm so used to being the last one here," as he turned out the lights to the bullpen on me. The bullpen was a maze of cubicles arranged on the lower level. If you picture a tri-level with an open view of the lower level, that's how the office was set up.

Harry turned the lights off on me at least four or five times before he'd finally started yelling, "Bart, you still down there?" Then finally he'd just say, "See you tomorrow, Bart!"—having learned that I'd most likely be the last to leave on any given night early in my career.

Things had gone from bad to worse at the office. Gerry was acting funny, and he wasn't around nearly as much as usual. He wasn't really talking with his agents on a regular basis, as we had all become used to him doing. I had caught wind of a rumor that he'd cut a special commission deal for his top three agents. He did have a fourth, but she had just left to open her own office on the other side of town. So, I guess as a way to tether the remaining three top agents, he gave them a bigger split.

I was still up and coming by the end of 2003. I was knocking on the door of being considered in the same breath as the remaining top producers, but I didn't get a commission raise. So when my good friend and colleague left to open a Re/Max, it was a time for a change. I was feeling slighted, and Gerry was acting aloof.

Prior to blindsiding Gerry on that Saturday morning, I had visited all of my twenty-seven listings and had had them sign a letter stating they wanted their listing to follow me to Re/Max. I had also looked up the broker state ID number and prefilled the entire transfer paperwork. All I needed was his signature.

"Hey, Gerry. How's it going?" I said nervously.

"Fine, Bart. How are you?" Gerry said without looking up from his desk.

"I think it's time for a change. I'm gonna make a switch to another company."

"Re/Max?" he said despondently.

I nodded.

"I figured it was just a matter of time. Are you sure about this, Bart? She has no clue how to run an office. It's a completely different ballgame than just being an agent," he said.

"Yeah, it's just not the same around here. I'm in need of a fresh start." Gerry's face reddened after my statement. He had a legendary temper.

"Here's a letter from each of my listing clients, and the state transfer form."

"OK, I don't know my broker number, so I'll have to get back to you with the form," he countered.

"I was able to find it and fill it in for you. All I need is your signature," I said, hoping he'd sign so I could get the hell outta there!

"Looks like you've thought of everything," he said with a hint of sarcasm.

He signed. I extended my hand, and he shook it. "Thanks, Gerry," I said. "I just won a bet with Tezak!"

"What bet?"

"Mike said you wouldn't shake my hand!"

"Haha. Good luck, Bart."

"You want to help me move my stuff outta the office?" I joked.

"You're pushing it, Bart!" He returned to his desk.

I spent the next hour walking boxes out to my car. Once the news was delivered I felt both relieved and apprehensive at the same time. I was leaving familiar for unknown. It would not be until years later that I discovered that in order to grow in life, you must get uncomfortable.

With my car packed with files, pictures, notebooks, and other assorted junk that you accumulate at an office, I pulled into the parking lot of Re/Max. My new home. A real turning point in my career. It wouldn't hurt that the market was about to catch fire!

The new Broker had always been one of my favorites. She was about ten years older than me but cool as hell!

She had been a top producer in the market for many years. She was a hustler, worked very hard, and always had a phone plastered to her ear. Kim was heavily recruited by the Re/Max Corporation and was finally talked into buying a franchise.

Right away she got a handful of well-respected agents to join the office including legendary Jim Powell, who became a good friend and mentor of mine. Nick and Rick joined as well. Nick DiToro and Rick Lahey were a team before teams became popular. They were very well respected midlevel producers.

Ann, of course, followed and became the office manager and minority owner.

Jane Kubal and Mike Tezak both hit the ground running after fleeing Century 21. Mike and I had become good buddies and were both on an upward trajectory. With me, Mike became the best recruiter! He would call me every day and say, "Get yer ass over here! It's awesome!"

I was probably secretly hoping for Gerry to put his arm around me and say, "You know, Bart, you're a real asset here and probably my favorite agent. I'd love it if you made your career here." Of course that never happened, but as you can tell from my dad stories, I was always unknowingly desperate for a male role model.

At Re/Max my business took off! In 2004 I earned $345,000—the most money I'd ever earned in a year!

At the end of 2004, I did what I always do at the end of the year. I always took a day or at least a half day to reflect on the previous year and set goals for the next one. As I sat in my "home office" in the basement of our house, I wrote out my goals. The list had ten items on it.

One of the goals was to make $500,000. Now that was a stretch. I had just come off my best year ever earning $345,000, and now I was crazy enough to set a goal to increase my income by 45 percent!

After setting my goals I put the notebook in the closet of my home office. I planned on returning to review the goals, but I did not (not recommended). The year flew by, and at the end of 2005 it was once again time to set my goals.

I returned to the closet and grabbed my goal-setting notebook. I reviewed my goals for 2005 and could not believe it. I had accomplished nine out of the ten goals. I rushed down to show Stacey the list. She laughed, rolled her eyes, and said, "Imagine that."

My income for 2005 was $509,000!

Again, any "accomplishment" that I mention is not to brag or say *look at me*. It's to first tell the story, and second to prove that (almost) anyone can do it.

One of my favorite movies of all-time is *Rudy*, which is based on a true story. Rudy is a lifelong Notre Dame football fan, and his goal is to make the team. He tries out for the team and gets his butt kicked. But the coach likes his hustle, and he keeps Rudy on the team on the practice squad. The practice squad is basically guys that help the real team get better at practice, kind of like real-life tackling dummies.

After a year and half of getting battered around on the practice squad, Rudy hears rumors that the coach may let him "dress" for a game. This means he gets to wear a uniform and stand on the sidelines. Before each game for the first few weeks of the season his senior year, Rudy diligently checks the list. He finally gets so frustrated with not dressing for a game that he quits. The janitor he had befriended and worked for his freshman year finds out about it and says this to Rudy…

"Since when are you the quitting kind?…So you didn't make the dress list. There are greater tragedies in the world…Oh, you are so full of crap. You're five feet nothin', one hundred and nothin', and you got hardly a speck of athletic ability. And you hung in with the best college football team in the land for two years. And you're also gonna walk outta here with a degree from the University of Notre Dame. In this lifetime, you don't have to prove nothin' to nobody—except yourself. And after what you've gone through, if you haven't done that by now, it ain't gonna never happen. Now go on back…"

I love that damn movie! I cry every time I watch it!

My point is that I'm an average (at best) looking guy, from a broken home, not overly intelligent, with tons of self-doubt, and I started out completely broke! If I can do it…you certainly can!

CHAPTER 21

Where'd All The Dough Go?

O
K, so everything's great, right? I had just had my biggest income year ever in 2005 earning $509,000!

Now what? I'll tell you what. We spent it! We did what most all red-blooded Americans do. As soon as you start making more money…you start spending more money!

There was a Princeton study done in 2010 regarding the correlation between money and happiness. The findings were that happiness does indeed increase to a small degree consistently all the way up to $75,000. Then it plateaus.

The study says that our emotional well being, or the pleasure we derive from day-to-day activities doesn't get any better after the household income reaches roughly $75,000.

Back in 2005, I didn't freaking know this! Coming from being a broke joke, I was driven by the pursuit of money. Or at least I thought it was at the time. Later I determined it was more my burning desire to not be broke anymore, and then never again. Finally, I've realized it's all about providing a stable environment for my family. Financial and relational.

Here's the rub! At the end of 2005, we had about ten thousand dollars in the bank. Sure, we put some money away in retirement accounts and some more on down payments for rental properties, but as far as getting our hands on some dough, jumping in the white Bronco, and heading out on the 405…we had only socked away $10K.

*If you're confused by the white Bronco thing, go to YouTube and search it!

You probably don't feel it, most people don't, but the reality is that we have way more things than we need in this country. After the basic necessities of food, clothing, and shelter, we have a lot of discretionary income.

We had a very simple economy and existence all the way up until the Industrial Revolution. Then all of a sudden we became very proficient at producing things. The big wigs and owners of these industrial companies had a looming problem, employees. They needed people with enough education to be average and with a background of following instructions and orders. This need led to our modern educational system.

The industries became very influential with the government. The government then built schools according to the desires of the industries. Follow orders, do what you're told, color within the lines, and we'll provide you with a living and eventually a retirement.

Once we became efficient at producing workers, the factories became even more proficient at producing things, which produced another problem. People didn't yet know they needed all of these things. These industries then became very good at marketing. The marketing led to the purchase of the new car, nice clothes, a home, a bigger home, a second car, etc.

Once the Jones's showed up with it, everyone else followed.

OK, I got on a little tangent there. Back to my spending, lol.

By 2008 we had a 4,200 square-foot house on forty acres, a condo in a gated community on the second green of a golf course in Bonita Springs, Florida, a Corvette convertible, a BMW, and a tricked out minivan with 2 drop-down DVD players and satellite TV!

I rarely drove the Corvette, and we visited the condo twice a year, which was great at first, but then I realized our kids only knew Indiana and southwest Florida…nothing else. We were compelled to vacation there because of the ongoing expense of owning the damn place!

Late in 2008, I inadvertently opened a credit card bill. My eyes nearly popped out of my head! The balance read $38,000!

How the hell could that be? We were doing so well, weren't we? We were definitely having a great time; I know that for sure. But at what expense?

Stacey and I sat down and discussed the credit card bill. Sure most of it was business expenses, but my name was still the one of the statement. We made a plan to get our shit together. It seemed like only days later that the stock market crashed followed by the economy.

We worked diligently on the credit card balance and had it paid off in about a year. Now we have it paid in full automatically each and every month. We've not carried a dime in credit card debt since.

In 2011 we sold the condo, the BMW, and the Corvette. I'm a slow learner I guess. In August of 2011, I paid cash for a 2008 Jeep Grand Cherokee Laredo. It had 26,000 miles on it and set the precedent for our rest-of-life car rule: buy used and pay cash.

The $38,000 credit card debt wasn't the first time we overextended ourselves with the plastic devil. It was the third!

In 2000, we racked up $27,000 in CC debt due, in large part, to my foray into full-time real estate. We did a cash-out refinance of our home and paid it off. Hindsight being what it is, this method is not recommended.

By the end of 2002, we had already repeated the *never do that again* lesson we thought we learned in 2000, cranking the CC debt up to $32,000. We sat down, made a plan, and slowly paid it off.

Our takeaway is simple yet lifechangingly (I may have just made that word up!) profound. It consists of two critical elements.

1. Make a plan. Anytime Stacey and I put our heads together and come up with a plan, we are incredibly productive. Whether is it's eliminating credit card debt, funding the kids, or selling our Dairy Queen, whenever we plan, we achieve.

2. Don't buy things. That's a broad blanketing statement, and it's one we haven't completely bought into (not Stacey anyway!) yet...it is, however, life changing. We are programmed from a very young age to consume. Buy this car and feel powerful, buy this watch and feel rich, buy this dress and feel sexy. Buy, buy, buy! Haha, that just reminded me of my favorite 'N Sync song! Anyway, our motto is: **We have nice things, but nice things don't have us!** They used to, but they don't now! We'd rather spend some dough on a nice vacation with all the kids than on a Rolex. **Spend on experiences—not on things!**

CHAPTER 22

Cheating Husband Rats Me Out!

My time at Re/Max was, for the most part, enjoyable. My production climbed each year that I was there.

In 2004 I sold fifty-eight homes and grossed $345,000. My team consisted of me, a full-time buyer's agent, and a part-time assistant. She worked twenty-five hours a week. I went on all of the listing appointments and about half of the buyer showings.

At Re/Max I had a ten by twelve foot office and one spot of the quad. The quad was an open space right next to my office with built-in countertops on both sides running the entire length of each wall, with larger surface areas at each corner. The corners made up each desk area.

I was on a ninety-five–five split and paid $1,110 per month for my office and $400 a month for the piece of the quad.

In 2005 we sold ninety-three homes and grossed $509,000.

In July we moved out of the Re/Max office and took our show on the road. By this time I represented a developer and all the builders of a 112-lot subdivision called Eagle Ridge. Mike Tezak and I had partnered in representing a 90-lot neighborhood called Abercrombie Woods. The streets were literally named after brands of clothing.

We had Aeropostle, Hilfiger, Abercrombie, etc.! What the hell? I thought. The neighborhood and the streets were named by the developer's wife, lol.

My team and I moved into one of the builder's spec homes that was to be used as a model and office. Our plan was to just move from home to home as we sold them. This turned out to be a crappy plan for several reasons.

One, we sold the homes too fast. We moved six times in six months. It was a nightmare and a complete pain in the ass! The team now consisted of two assistants, one full-time and one part-time, three buyer's agents, and me. We had a desk for everyone, filing cabinets, a bunch of computers, a decent-size copier, and everything else you could imagine…to schlep around from house to house.

Our desks were those inexpensive pressed wood jobbers you can get from Staples. I used a simple utility table. Putting the desks together each and every time, reassembling the computer stations, and relying on phone and Internet service providers all became too much to put up with.

This was also the time that I decided to become a homebuilder. The developer of Eagle Ridge was also a builder in the neighborhood. Right before we opened the lots up for construction I brought him a business plan. I would buy lots, finance the construction, build his models, and allow him to put his signs on my jobsites. He would supervise the construction utilizing his subs, and I'd pay him a flat fee for his efforts.

He immediately shot down the idea. "Why in the hell would I allow my agent to be a direct competitor in the home building business?" he snapped. "Think of it this way. I represent all of the builders in the neighborhood. Some are assholes. Their jobsites are a mess. You complain about them all the time to me. You continue to allow them to buy lots, because you need to sell lots. I'll be a great lot-buying customer; you can show my spec homes as your own, and you'll get a little sump'em sump'em on each house that I build," I countered.

Eventually he wrapped his mind around the idea and liked it. We ended up building two or three homes a year from 2005 to 2013. I stopped only because it became an unnecessary distraction, albeit a minor one.

You might think it's a conflict of interest for me to be building homes in a neighborhood where I represent every single one of the builders. It wasn't. I think I told you before that I have an uncanny way of being completely fair and equally effective in representing both sides of a transaction. The same applied to selling spec homes. In fact, I would always go out of my way to sell other builders' homes before mine. I believed in abundance then, and I believe in it more so now!

The homes we were building were anywhere between $250,000 to $300,000. On the building side of things we'd make around $25,000 net per house.

When phase two of Eagle Ridge was set to open, I put together a lot-selling event. Stacey helped me organize it. We rented a banquet room at the popular Strongbow Inn. We sent out beautiful invitations to our target builders.

I got Jack (the developer) to agree to pick up the tab for the food and open bar. We had our name tags ready when our esteemed builder guests arrived. At the entrance to the banquet room, we had one of our assistants acting as hostess. She would greet them, find their name tags, and then escort them to their seats where a *Reserved for Such and Such* placard was waiting.

I gave a quick presentation regarding the Phase II lots that included the exclusive Pond Lots and Wooded Perimeter Lots. The pond was an ill-planned retention pond with treacherously steep banks down to the water. The wooded lots backed up to a preserve. It turned out this wasn't a nature preserve but a wetland preserve that got a little marshy and filled with mosquitos from time to time. We really didn't know any of this at the time.

The dirt was being moved in Phase II, but nothing was finished. The developer had been led astray a bit by the engineering firm that designed the neighborhood.

After my presentation I asked who would be reserving lots on this night. A dozen builders raised their hands out of the fifteen in the crowd. Yahtzee! I thought. Stacey then helped me put the preprinted names of the participating builders into a glass fishbowl, and we dug them out one at a time.

The rules were simple; we set it up just like my fantasy football team. We picked out the builder names in order of their *draft* position. The first name out of the bowl got the first lot choice, and so on. We proceeded this way until we reached pick number twelve, then the selection order snaked.

This meant that builder twelve got the twelfth pick and the thirteenth. We snaked back and forth until each builder had picked up enough lots for their appetite or budget.

We sold forty lots that night! The average sales price was $55,000 per lot. Jack sat in the far corner by himself sipping scotch with a Cheshire grin on his face.

By the spring of 2006, Jack was moving dirt in a brand new neighborhood about five miles away called Timberland. This development would consist of 153 home sites and would be another huge success.

In the summer we moved our office to one of my spec homes in Timberland, where we stayed until winter. I decided we'd use the home as a model and office, but it wouldn't be for sale. In October we had a really hot buyer that insisted we sell her the house.

I agreed and decided that moving from house to house was no longer viable for the size of the team. We were up to two full-time assistants, five "production" agents, and me. I renamed them production assistants because I knew one day my vision was to be completely out of the appointment side of the business. I just didn't realize how long it would actually take!

In the meantime, somewhere around fall of 2005, the Broker packed up and moved to Appleton, Wisconsin. Her husband had an opportunity to run a brand-new state-of-the-art heart clinic. He jumped at the chance and Kim of course followed.

I remember her calling me on a Saturday morning. I was walking the streets of the busily under construction Phase II of Abercrombie Woods. I wanted to make sure the spec homes my team was holding open that day were ready to go.

"Listen, you're the first person I'm telling this to, so please keep it to yourself for now," she confided.

Wow this must be something big! I thought.

"Dave and I are moving to Wisconsin. In fact, he's is already there."

"Wow! Is that good news?"

"Well, the timing sucks, but it's a great opportunity for him," she said sounding unsure. "I love Valpo, and I've got the real estate company doing pretty well and all…but it's gonna be a good move for us I think."

"So what are going to do with Re/Max?" I asked cluelessly.

"Well, that's why I'm calling you. Would you and Stacey be interested in buying the business?"

Oh my God, bombshell! "Uh, wow…I really haven't ever even considered it. I thought someday I would definitely own my own company, but we've been so busy…I don't know."

"You and Stacey talk it over. In the meantime I'm going to talk to Ann about it. I'm sure she's not interested. And if she is, she'd probably be very interested in having you as a partner. She does have a 20 percent profit-only ownership interest. I'm not sure how that applies when I sell the business."

"What's a profit-only ownership interest?"

"It means Ann gets 20 percent of the net profits produced by the business but none of the expense or losses."

Wow, what a deal. Ann, that wily gal, had negotiated a helluva deal!

I rushed home and broke the news to Stacey. "How'd you like to buy Re/Max?" I asked.

"What are talking about, Bubba?"

"She and Doc are moving to Wisconsin, and she wants us to buy the company."

"For how much?"

She didn't even flinch. This wasn't the risk-averse Stacey I knew!

"Not sure, we didn't get that far. She asked me to talk it over with you and get back to her."

"You said someday you'd own your own company. Maybe your chance is already here?" she said calmly.

Monday I didn't hear from her. I was getting excited thinking of all the possibilities! On Tuesday I called her. "Hey, it's Bart, what's happening?" I was trying to contain my excitement.

"We just left a meeting with the attorney. It seems as though Ann has a first right of refusal. I'm still pretty sure she won't want to buy it, but I will check with her and let you know."

"Sounds good! Stace and I talked. We're interested!"

"Awesome Bart. I'd feel great leaving the company in the hands of two of my favorite people!" She was always a great salesperson.

Turns out her assistant wanted to exercise her first right to purchase, and she already had a built-in 20 percent ownership, so she was buying at a discount.

So at the end of 2006 I was negotiating a deal to come back into the office with ample office space. We worked out a deal for $45,000 in *desk fees* and a ninety-nine–one split. The one percent is for Re/Max International.

The $45,000 sounds like a lot, but it's not considering the amount of commissions I was starting to bring in. I now had four private offices, the quad, and a small private conference room. Ann had to move all the agents around to accommodate me. As if they weren't already jealous of my production, now they got uprooted and told to move to the other side of the building.

In 2006 we sold 115 homes and brought in $612,000 in commission.
In 2007 we sold 129 homes and totaled $695,000 in commission.
In 2007 we also went bananas with our investments. Over the years we started to acquire small single-family homes for the rental income and long-term appreciation.

In February of 2007, I went alone to a Dave Lindahl seminar in downtown Chicago. We live about an hour away from downtown. Dave's seminar was all about buying apartment buildings. He had a great presentation, and I bought his $795 information product, which consisted of a couple of binders and a bunch of audio CDs. It turned out to be one of my best investments ever!

In August we closed on a fifty-two-unit complex in Rensselaer for $2.2 million. The process was very stressful. I really didn't know what I was doing, and I had nobody around to advise me. I remember we spent a few weeks at our condo in Florida that summer, and I was running back and forth to the library to print out e-mails and contracts and loan docs to sign…and to Office Max to fax back and forth.

I'll save the details of this particular complex for its own book. Let me just preface it by saying it was a government-subsidized development, a nonstop Jerry Springer show. I had no real idea what white trash was until we took over those apartments!

At the end of September we closed on twenty-four more units, this time in Valpo right off Lincolnway at the end of a cul-de-sac.

In December my first buyer's agent, who became a good friend and by this time is my next-door neighbor in Bartopia, talked me into investing in a Dairy Queen with her and her husband Jeff.

Oh and did I mention Stacey gave birth to Bart II on November 28, 2007? We were out of control! The truth is, I was out of control! Stacey is averse to risk, or at least she was, lol!

Needless to say, 2007 flew by and I left most of the day-to-day real estate sales stuff up to the team. And they did an excellent job!

In 2007 we sold 129 homes and brought in $695,000 in commission.

To add a little more to a wild year, in August I talked the new owner into selling me the company. We negotiated back and forth and came to an agreed upon price. She was going to stay on as manager, and we were going to open offices all over Northwest Indiana.

But something happened the night my son was born that changed my mind. She made a bad judgment call. Looking back I see that it wasn't a huge deal, but given my ego at the time I wouldn't let her off easy. So I killed the deal! I'll give you all of the details in a future book.

Soon after we had a team meeting, and I explained everything to them. I've always been blessed by having a great team around me, especially my OG buyer's agent, Cindy Malmquist, and my longtime assistant, Karlene Hampton. We treat them like family, and in return we get the same.

In this meeting I asked their opinion: Should we stay or should we go? Leaving would mean pulling up the stakes and opening my own independent company.

After the sale imploded, I tried to talk her into letting me have a satellite office like we use to have in the spec homes. I even told her I'd go back to a ninety-five–five split and pay a $1,000 desk fee even though I wouldn't have a desk. She turned me down and said corporate had told her no. Later I spoke with corporate and they had never had a conversation with Ann about it. I understood though. She was just trying to keep her biggest cash cow in house paying the big desk fee.

The team voted on leaving Re/Max and going independent. It was a good thing, because Stacey and I had already made up our minds. We were leaving! Stacey and I didn't spend much time in the office from the time

Deuce was born through the holidays. In late January we had a team meeting for lunch at Red Robin. The whole team was there: assistants Dawn and Karlene; agents Cindy, Sandi, Peggy, and Dave. At lunch Stacey and I made the announcement that we were leaving to open our own company. Everyone cheered! We left the restaurant at one thirty.

By 4:00 p.m. an e-mail went out to the entire company from the Broker. It said that I would no longer be a part of Re/Max Affiliates. What the hell? I thought. That ass head Dave had run and told her everything! Dave was a new agent on my team. It was kind of weird, because he came to my team from another team within the office. She had talked me into taking him on. Soon after Dave joined the team, the agent whose team he left also asked to join my team. The Broker begged me not to take her, because then she'd lose that agent's monthly desk fee.

What a dick! I took this guy into the family, and he double-crossed me!

In the e-mail to the office she told everyone that I'd be out by the following Friday. I'm not sure why she gave me a week, but it worked out perfectly.

Stacey and I had just purchased a retail strip center on Route 30. Route 30 is the main east and west thoroughfare that runs through town. We had already begun remodeling the only vacant unit out of the five in the building. The rehab now had to go into overdrive!

She also wasn't going to release any of my fifty-two listings until we returned each and every one of her lockboxes and had every t crossed and i dotted in our pending files. She also refused to sign my state transfer until said items were completed.

We called a meeting with the CEO of our local Board of Realtors and explained our situation. She said no problem; she'd help us out. We signed the transfer paperwork without her signature and overnighted it to Indianapolis with a letter stating she refused to sign.

In the meantime, the CEO of the Board entered us into the MLS as a new company effective right then and there and assigned us new lockboxes to take with us. Our concern, of course, was removing the old lockboxes from all of our listings and that no showings could be accommodated while we waited to get the new boxes. This interesting twist allowed us to make one trip to each listing and make a quick swap.

As I sat in a secretary's office going through each and every new lockbox and initialing a form confirming the serial numbers, another gal came racing back panicked.

"She keeps calling, and she's pissed! You guys better hurry and get out of here!" she said sounding out of breath.

I probably haven't mentioned it yet, but she was the president of the MLS at the time! She noticed right away, or else one of her lackeys pointed out to her that Bart Vickrey & Co Real Estate popped up in the MLS as a new company!

The Friday of my deadline to get out had arrived. We had movers rolling hard starting at 8:00 a.m. Their job was to get all of the big stuff moved from our offices at Re/Max to the newly remodeled home of Bart Vickrey & Co Real Estate.

That was one of the weirdest days of my life! It was like dead man walking! We were moving stuff out forever, while the rest of the agents tried to go about their daily business.

Around three thirty we met and returned all of her lockboxes. She went through every page of every pending file that we had neatly lined up for her review.

The meeting adjourned, and I forced a hug on her. She reluctantly accepted. Looking back now I feel bad that things turned out the way they did, not for me but for her. I'm sure I dumped a lot of undue stress on her at that time.

Dave left town about a year later. He and his also married mistress moved to Arizona together leaving both their spouses in the dust. I knew that jackass was having an affair! He had this builder client that was a woman. She seemed manlier than him even though he was a big lug of a man.

I remember visiting her spec home during a Parade of Homes when Dave was on my team. That night I told Stacey something's up with Dave and the Lady Builder (I can't for the life of me think of her name right now!).

Anyway, I had four good years at Re/Max. That Broker and I are now once again friends. Unfortunately Re/Max closed its doors a little over two years after we left.

CHAPTER 23

In 2009 I Made $100!

I knew we had a rough year in 2009, but I was shocked at the reality of it. Stacey and I stared at the profit and loss statement in disbelief. Bart Vickrey & Co Real Estate had total net profits of $100 in 2009!

My business model is a little different than most. It's just me and my team of a handful of agents and a couple assistants.

We sold seventy-two homes in 2009. That's a lot! So, why didn't we make a profit? It didn't take long to figure it out!

Two things: Our marketing budget was still based on the robust market of 2005, and I had my head up my ass!

I spent very little time working in or on my real estate sales business that year. My team handled all the leads, went on all the appointments, and I took very little accountability.

Starting in late 2008, right after the stock market tanked, finally buckling to the tidal wave of shit created by the collapse of the real estate market, I decided to start a real estate investment fund. The idea, of course, was brilliant: pool together a bunch of people's money and buy up as much distressed real estate as possible.

I hired this guy out of Atlanta named Clark Gray to coach me through the process. His fee was $7,000. He talked me into coming down to a conference he was hosting called The Money Hunt. It was for people with business ideas in need of funding or partners or both. Mark introduced me to a securities attorney. I ended up hiring him to draft the Offering Memorandum, which is legally necessary to raise money for these types of ventures. The Memorandum cost me $15,000, and he said it was a discount because I knew Clark. Some discount, I thought!

One of the speakers at the conference was Dick Simon (not his real name), former Managing Director of the New York Stock Exchange. After his speech, I spoke to Dick at a little wine mixer that was held after day two of the conference. We hit it off and he said he really liked my idea.

He also said he represented a group of Chinese investors looking to be involved in American real estate.

As the cocktails continued, we had a group of about ten people yucking it up and having a good ole time. We decided to make our way over to the hotel bar to continue the party and get some food.

To my left was an attractive, gregarious gal, probably mid to late forties. She was also the owner of one of Chicago's biggest strip clubs. To my right was this flamboyant Italian guy. I can't remember his name exactly, but I think it was Vito. He was svelte, well dressed, completely bald, and I'm guessing around forty years old.

By this time, Dick was having such a good time that he called the airline and canceled his flight back to New York and booked an extra night at the hotel. We were having a great time when suddenly I feel a hand on my knee. I quickly calculated in my head that it's my left knee thus eliminating the possibility of Vito's man paw violating my personal space. But I was still frozen without a clear thought of what to do next. I slowly turned my head, and she was staring at me with beaming eyes and a wide smile.

I'd like to say this kind of stuff happens to me all the time, but you've seen my profile picture. It doesn't! She leaned in with her lips close enough to my ear that I could feel her hot breath and said, "This is for you." She handed me a folded scrap of paper. When I opened it I found four scrawled digits. Still staring down at the paper, she then whispered, "That's my room number. Come see me tonight." All that I could muster at that very moment was, "Wow!"

Abruptly, I excused myself for the bathroom. It was true. I did have to go. After using the can, I called my wife, Stacey. "Hey babe, how's it going there?" I said.

"Oh, pretty good, just about to put your son to bed. Girls are up in their rooms."

"You are not going to believe this!" Quickly I told her the story of the woman and the room number.

"Oh my God, what a whore," Stacey said. "You told her you were happily married, right?" she demanded.

"Well, it didn't really come up, but I'm wearing my wedding ring. I'm not sure that she cares," I offered.

"What are you going to do?" she asked.

As I began to describe my elaborate escape plan, Stacey yelled, "I gotta call you back. Deuce is choking on a piece of carpet!" And she hung up. My son, Bart II, is nicknamed Deuce. When he was an infant he liked to crawl around on his belly and pick threads of carpeting from the living room rug and eat them. He would choke from time to time.

She called back about twenty minutes later, "So what'd you tell that slut?" she quizzed. "Uhm, nothing," I said.

"What do you mean nothing? Are you still at the bar?" she asked.

"No, I'm in my room. After you hung up I snuck to the elevators and made my escape!" I answered.

"You didn't tell them you were leaving?" she said, sounding relieved. Then there was a knock at the door.

"Hold on. Someone's at the door."

"Oh my God, it's that bitch! Do not open that door!" she screamed. I flung open the door and ushered it in with delight. I couldn't wait to get my hands on it!

"Don't worry. It's just room service with my calamari and two bottles of Miller Lite," I laughed.

On Tuesday of the following week I got a call at my office. It was Dick Simon. We had a great conversation. He went on to tell me that the

Chinese may have interest in my real estate investment fund. Dick wanted to fly in from New York and spend the day with me.

I couldn't believe it! I was so excited I could barely contain myself.

The following Tuesday Dick arrived. I was so nervous that I was pacing the office with anticipation. He was a very affable guy and quickly put me at ease.

We had lunch at Applebee's, and he told me, "Bart, I'm very impressed with you. You're gonna make a great CEO."

"Thank you. I'm very excited about the opportunity we have in this market," I said.

"I'm going to be able to help you raise a lot of money for your fund" he assured me. "However, I think you need to raise the threshold to fifty million!"

Oh my God, this guy must be crazy. Crazy awesome! Up until this time, my idea for the investment fund was to raise two million in cash and leverage it through financing. Now this guy was talking about fifty million? This was nuts!

"What you'll find, Bart, is it's easier to raise big money than little money. The Chinese wouldn't feel comfortable with a small fund. So, we need to go big," he said expertly.

We got back to my office and talked some more. He finally broke the ice on his fee. The fee was $4,000 per month and 10 percent of the company. This guy could have said just about anything, and I'd have agreed.

Somehow I was able to get him down to 5 percent…but in hindsight, I should have negotiated his damn consulting fee.

He left and I got an e-mail the next morning with wiring instructions for the first month's fee. It was wired by noon the same day. We talked later in the afternoon for about twenty minutes. He said my business plan needed to be revised and I needed a nice website to send would-be investors to. He had just the guy.

The next day I was on the phone with the web designer, and he was describing this incredible website with a dramatic flash introduction equipped with sound and then a pulsing logo with the sound of a heartbeat. The name of my first real estate fund was Heartland Fund I. I'm from the Midwest. Some call it the Heartland of America…you do the math. Anyway, the price tag was five grand down and five grand upon completion.

No problem, I thought, after all we were all going to make millions with this business, and I was going to make the investors even richer than they already were! It took a little over a month for the site to be completed. In the meantime, I was talking to Dick about three or four hours per week. How in the world can that be worth $4,000 per month?

OK, to try to salvage your interest and make the long story short, Dick never did produce a viable investor. I put an end to the "consulting" deal only after four months of wasted time and money. To my dismay, I had basically been duped by all parties involved. I was so caught up in the idea of building this incredible investment company and making tons of dough that I was blind to reason.

Money coach $7,000. Offering memorandum $15,000. Website $10,000. Consulting $16,000. Miscellaneous $3,000. The venture cost a whopping grand total of $51,000! Of course, while chasing this crazy idea, I wasn't paying attention to my core business—real estate sales.

So, I got what I deserved! $100 net profit from Bart Vickrey & Co Real Estate, and $51,000 down the drain for the Heartland Fund!

I've rambled a little long, but I wanted to set up my real estate rebirth story, which you will find in the next chapter. See you then!

CHAPTER 24

Rebirth 2010

I n 2010 I reentered my business. After making a whopping one hundred dollars from Bart Vickrey Real Estate in 2009, it was up to me to right the ship.

My plan was to get into the Internet lead business, go after expired listings, and any other business-producing pillar I could find and then build into my day-to-day operations.

So I started looking specifically for companies in the Internet lead generation space.

In June after searching through a handful of similar companies I found Real Geeks. Real Geeks is an all in one solution for agent and broker websites, CRM, and lead generation. I already had a good website through Web Agent Solutions (which I've had since 2007 and still utilize as my branded lead capture website). I was already using Top Producer, which, in my opinion, is the best CRM system available for agents.

I wanted Real Geeks specifically for the Internet buyer lead generation and capture. During my research I looked into Tiger Leads, Boomtown, and Market Leader. What impressed me most about Real Geeks was Jeff Manson. Jeff is the founder of Real Geeks and is a practicing real estate broker. We had a couple of conversations and his enthusiasm was conta-gious. Real Geeks had an immediate impact on my business and now, over five years later, still consistently produces over six figures in commissions directly into my business each and every year.

Since I've become a customer of Real Geeks, they have continued to improve the product. They now have a great seller lead generation platform available as well. It's been working out for us.

So now that I had an Internet buyer lead system in place, I wanted to develop and implement an expired marketing plan. By 2010 I had been in the business over ten years full-time and had not once had any consistent expired marketing plan in place.

Back in 2008 I had hired Kinder Reese as my one-on-one coach. Unfortunately the timing wasn't great, because that was also around the time I started dreaming and then chasing my real estate investment fund idea. So I didn't last very long the first time around with them, but they had an immediate impact on my business.

On my very first coaching call with Jay Kinder he said, "Do you charge a processing fee in your business?"

"No."

"Well, you need to start charging one immediately!" he said with his Oklahoman accent. "I'm serious, Bart. You have to charge a processing fee."

"Uh, well…I don't know…," I stammered.

Then he made it real simple for me. "Do you do more for your clients than the average agent in your marketplace?" he quizzed.

"A lot more!" I said proudly.

"Then, there ya go!"

He was right! And I never forgot that, even though I wasn't smart enough to really make it part of my business model until a couple years later.

In 2010 we got serious about the processing fee. And we have collected well over $200,000 in processing fees since. Thanks, Jay Kinder and Mike Reese!

That's not all I have to thank them for. It was Mike Reese's expired marketing campaign that I invested in around September of 2010. I had it running by November and made an extra $87,000 with it in 2011. We've changed some of the copywriting messages and added two more sales letters to the plan since then, but it was Mike's idea that inspired the whole thing. In the five years that we've been consistently running the campaign, we've added over $500,000 to our bottom line!

You can get copies of our expired campaign at www.realestategoodlife. com. It's free, no strings attached.

Along with the expired direct mail campaign we also utilize The RedX and Top Producer. The RedX is a no-brainer investment. Their software reaches into the MLS and pulls all the expired listings out for me and then checks the Internet for phone numbers. It's dirt cheap and saves a ton of time.

In Top Producer we built out a marketing plan that reminds us who to send which mailing to and on which day of the week. It's very easy to customize marketing plans within TP. The RedX spits out the list, I mark the expireds that I want to mail to, one of my assistants enters them into TP and launches the Expired Program. When it's time for each mailing to go out, she gets a task assigned to her dashboard in TP. Like I said, it's very simple. And if you already have TP and want to copy it just let me know. You can write me at bart@bartsellshouses.com or text me at 219-405-3768.

Now I had two legitimate money-making lead generation pillars in place. It was time to install the next one!

I've been a customer of Gary Elwood's over at Proquest Technologies since 2006. His company provides trackable toll-free numbers to use to monitor your advertising. When somebody calls in response to an ad, Proquest records his or her phone number and then texts and e-mails you a notification. You can track specific ads right down to the exact listing or buyer offer you've attached with the toll-free number. We use the toll-free numbers for our property flyers and Craigslist ads, specifically, but we have also used them for Facebook, *Homes* magazine, sign riders, bandit signs, etc.

In 2010 I got serious again about the utilization of the toll-free numbers and have had a return on investment of over fifty times! This is not a misprint! I've had an ongoing fifty-plus times return on investment.

In case you're wondering, I do not get any kickbacks, referral fees, or other perks from any of the companies that I'm mentioning in this chapter. I just wanted to give you some of the specific systems, campaigns, and processes that we are using today in our business.

Also in 2010, I bought an inexpensive Craigslist program called Buyer Leads by Tonight through Josh Shoenly and Retechulous.com. The system was very simple to implement and started to produce immediate results. Since then I've bought a number of programs from Josh and Retechulous. They're highly recommended.

We then added another layer and coupled the ideas from Josh and the technology from ProQuest, which added another consistent stream of leads, essentially for free from Craigslist. The Craigslist lead is a very low converting lead, but I look at it two ways. One, if you produce enough and sift enough, the legitimate buyers do surface. The other is that we should be building lists of people at all times. With Craigslist, I am able to consistently add to my e-mail list all the time.

Last year we brought in $98,000 from the Craigslist program we tweaked and measure all the time. You can get the thirteen-page PDF outline of the step-by-step process on the website as well: www.realestategood-life.com.

I figured that if I put every step to every marketing program that I'm listing here for you, this book would be six hundred pages long…and I know then you'd have never bought it! So I can send you to the website where everything is electronically held and delivered. I know that only the most serious practitioners will take the steps necessary to collect everything…and then only a whisper of a percentage of those agents will actually take the time to build and deploy the systems into their businesses… whew, I'm outta breath, but you get the idea!

To put your mind at ease, everything I mention and direct you to is absolutely FREE on the website, no strings attached, no smoke and mirrors, no hocus-pocus!

In October of 2010, I flew down to Plano, Texas, for the Kinder Reese Exponential Growth Summit. The night before the conference Jay Kinder and Mike Reese had organized a mixer in the hotel lounge. I met two very interesting people that night.

The first was Lars Hedenborg. Lars is an agent in Charlotte, North Carolina. When I met him he was on pace to sell one hundred homes that year. He now sells over four hundred a year! My conversations with Lars over the couple of days at the seminar were completely different than most agent conversations that I'm used to having. I could tell he was on pace to become a superstar agent. Talking to Lars was inspiring. He isn't the usual emotional, high-energy type you think of in a top-producing agent. He's very matter-of-fact and businesslike in the way he speaks and describes his approach and philosophy. He's a super intelligent guy.

During the conference several of the speakers either had products or books to sell. I noticed that Lars would join in line to purchase something every time. Finally, I approached him while he stood in line for yet another product.

"Hey, Lars, you're buying that too?"

Looking at me with all seriousness, he said, "Bart, I buy everything."

I finally found an agent that invests more than I did on books, coaching, programs, audio CDs, etc.!

Lars still has his high-producing real estate sales business, but he's also now started coaching agents. I bought one of his products, and it was excellent! It was all about systems, tracking, and specific lead generation. Check him out!

That first night in the hotel lounge I also met a guy wearing a shirt that said Billion Dollar Agent. I recognized the name and logo. I went up to him and said, pointing to the logo on his shirt, "I read that book!"

"Hey, that's great. I'm the author, Steve Kantor!" he said proudly.

We had a great conversation, and I could tell right away this guy was special.

The first day of the conference was great, one mind-blowing presentation after the next. Lunchtime was there before I knew it. Sitting to my right were a couple of really nice guys from Canada, a father and son real estate team. We had made quick plans to have lunch together.

As I wheeled to exit my row, there was Steve. "Hey, Bart, you wanna grab lunch?"

"Sure, if you don't mind Bill and Michael coming with us."

"The more the merrier!" he answered.

We scrambled out of the Marriott Hotel and walked down to a nice restaurant where we were seated outside. Steve then began to drop bombshells! He was like a real estate mad scientist! And he's not even an agent!

Steve is an author of a couple of real estate books. One of the books is called *Billion Dollar Agent Manifesto*. It's a must read! You'll learn more about the books and his company Best Agent Business later.

Anyway, Steve said something during that lunch that I've kept in mind ever since. He said, "You guys should only be doing one of three things!"

1. Meeting with Buyer, Sellers, and SOI (sphere of influence)
2. Calling Buyers, Sellers, and SOI
3. Other

"And other should be delegated to someone else as quickly possible!" he added.

I've tampered with the list since hearing it from Steve. I've added Marketing to Buyers, Sellers, and SOI as number two on the list, and I've moved the calling to number three. Plus, I don't like calling anyone, so I guess I had to delegate both numbers three and four on my list as quickly as possible!

Steve and I kept in touch after the conference and still talk from time to time. About a month after the conference, I hired his company, Best Agent Business, to help me organize my database, call my SOI, and hold my team members accountable.

My experience with Steve and Best Agent Business has been incredible. For anyone that is on the fence about hiring an assistant, check out his company right now!

He will have advice for you if you're not sure if you should hire, or if you can afford it, or if you'd know how to train someone, or if you have enough work for them to do (and I know this is probably you!).

At the conference I also heard Michael Mayer speak as he was releasing a book called *The Seven Levels of Communication*. He gave a great speech, and I bought his book and he signed it for me.

If you have not read the book, you must get it (and actually read it) immediately! The book is written in a story format, which always makes for easier and more entertaining reading. After reading his book, I implemented his idea of stacking, which is scheduling networking lunches and coffees back-to-back to back on a certain day of the week.

I used this method in 2011 coupled with the idea of building my own Business Referral Network…and it worked brilliantly! I don't have enough pages left in this book to describe the Business Referral Network and the impact it has had on my business, but I will say that my entire hefty monthly expense associated with our printed newsletter is completely covered by the advertising and sponsorships from the Network.

Read Michael's book and check out his program called Boost. I tried it and was blown away at the overall process involved. It's very simple and extremely effective.

Around dinnertime on the second day I joined up with a couple of dudes that have since become long-time friends, Matt O'Neill and Todd Tramonte.

Matt is an agent out of Charleston, South Carolina, and a great guy. If you have a referral for his area, do not hesitate to send them his way. Matt, I remember, was on pace to sell thirty-two homes that year. Now he and his team are approaching 50 million dollars a year in sales.

Todd Tramonte has an office in Richardson, Texas. He had just gotten rid of his Help-U-Sell discount franchise when I met him. He's a great family guy and works circles around his competition. Todd has the magical ability to collect over 7 percent commission on his listings, and he's worth every dollar! Todd now has a program available where he gives you a back-stage pass to his entire operations. It's a two-day, intense, all-hands-on-deck training program. Look him up!

I mention all these people, the relationships I've been able to develop, and the impact they've had on me for three reasons:

1. To give you the origin story on the lead generation and business systems that I use in my day-to-day business.

2. To illustrate that the teacher will appear when the student is looking, and more importantly, ready!

3. To, once again give a shout out and big thank you to Jay Kinder and Mike Reese for completely changing my real estate mind-set and putting me in the path of all these other great people!

Mike and Jay's business has since exploded and can now be found at NAEA.com.

I've been influenced by many people over my career. I've purchased programs, copied ideas, and been inspired by all of the people mentioned above and countless others over the years. Each time the key is the same. The information, coaching, advice, etc. means absolutely nothing without IMPLEMENTATION!

Here's a chronological overview of the influences I've had in real estate:

- 1999: Roger Butcher
- 2000: Craig Forte
- 2001: Mike Ferry (I found a training program he had on VHS tapes and watched them over and over again!)
- 2003: Brian Buffini (I had one-on-one coaching or self-paced coaching with his company for many years. His coaching is centered on the database…which is always priority #1.)
- 2004: Gary Keller and his book *The Millionaire Real Estate Agent*
- 2005: Craig Proctor (Craig completely changed the way I looked at real estate marketing. I still utilize a lot of his methodologies to this day)
- 2006: Gary Elwood and Proquest Technologies
- 2008: Jay Kinder and Mike Reese (I'm still following them to this day!)

- 2010: Jeff Manson with Real Geeks, Steve Kantor with Best Agent Business, Michael Mayer with the book *The Seven Levels of Communication*, Josh Shoenly with Retechulous, Lars Hedenborg, Matt O'Neill, and Todd Tramonte
- 2011: Pat Hiban and his book *6 Steps to 7 Figures* (a must read)
- 2012: Tom Ferry (Check out his videos on YouTube and go to one of his conferences!)
- 2013: Implementing our Good Life Tracker for daily accountability
- 2014: Dan Kennedy's advice to get an authentic printed newsletter out to my database
- 2015: Ryan Fletcher and his book *Defeat Mega-Agents* (This is funny, since I'm classified as a mega-agent!) I highly recommend his book and podcast.

Check out all these guys! Always be on the lookout for ways to better your life and business!

CHAPTER 25

Stacey and Bart Get Divorced?

At the beginning of the book, I started and did not finish this story. Much to Stacey's chagrin I even wrote about it in my newsletter that now goes out to over nine-hundred people.

Here's the article I published in the newsletter. In it you'll find the ending to the story.

I wanted to also show you what I mean by being authentic. Most people would not dare write an article about their marital problems. I did. The feedback was amazing.

From the newsletter:
How my obsession with NOT being broke nearly cost me my marriage...

A few newsletters ago I started a story with: "So we're lying in bed in our suite at the Excellence Playa Mujeres Resort in Mexico. The date is

December 8, 2012…the time is 1:15 a.m. Stacey (my wife) turns to me with her eyes filled with tears and says…"Maybe we should get a divorce…"

I thought maybe I should finish the story.

It may take a couple of newsletters to finish all of it…but here it goes…

When I heard Stacey mention the word divorce it was like getting splashed with a pail of ice cold water. Keep in mind that in the sixteen years (now seventeen) that we had been married this was literally the first time the word had come out of one of our mouths!

Now keep in mind the scenario: It was very late at night. We'd been traveling all day. And we were both soaked in alcohol. Whenever I partake of more than the legal limit, my DP (Dark Passenger) is involved in a lot of my decisions and actions.

*More on my Dark Passenger in upcoming newsletter. A brief definition: DP is the voice inside my head that influences some of my decisions and actions. He can be cold and to the point. He thinks more about me than about others. He's been great for business, bad for relationships, fun at parties, and a complete tool. He's been with me for as long as I can remember, but it wasn't until after this incident in Mexico that I really even gave DP much thought. Lately I've done a much, much better job controlling him, and not the reverse.

So, the love of my life whispers "maybe we should get a divorce"… and before I have a chance to respond, DP responds for me…"Maybe we should."

Fortunately, the topic sobered me up almost instantly, I was able to wrestle my voice box back from DP. I was able to stutter, "Why?" At that moment, my whole marriage flashed before me!

Stacey and I went on our first date on November 28, 1997. We were engaged on February 10, 1998. (I tried to wait until Valentine's Day, but I just couldn't.) We were married on August 22, 1998…and we had Madison on August 5, 1999.

We started fast and have packed a ton of incredible experiences and memories into our sixteen years together. I remember the overwhelming feeling of joy and happiness watching her walk down the aisle. I could barely see her through the tears in my eyes (just as I can barely see the keys on my MacBook as I write this story…wiping the tears so I can finish). I felt so lucky, so blessed, and so proud to have this wonderful woman in my life!

I remember the look on her face when Madison was born. This oversized thing (Madison) just came out of an undersized place. My mother was in the corner of the room on the brink of passing out, because, as she explained to us later, she empathized with the pain Stacey was going through.

So Madison popped out, and the first thing Stacey said was, "I'd do it again!"

What? Are you crazy? I just witnessed something that is so "natural" look so unnatural…yikes! And the first thing out of your mouth is that you'd do it again! And of course, we did! Two more times…with Maya in 2002, and Deuce (Bart II) in 2007.

Stacey was the person with enough faith in me to encourage my venture into full-time real estate sales in January of 2000. This was a no-turning-back leap of faith without safety net. She had the confidence in me when few others did.

She stood by me without wavering as I built the business. She worked around the clock (the first few years), held down the fort, and took care of me and the kids all while working full-time.

She was my hero. My Super Hero. My Wonder Woman.

She had my back…at all times. She was my witness. My witness, as in, she was there day by day as the one person that knew me best. She saw my struggles, knew my inner most thoughts, enjoyed my company, and laughed at my jokes.

How could it be that now she said, "Maybe we should get a divorce?"

It came down to a simple failure to communicate, a failure on both of our parts. And it came down to my unwavering, unrelenting fear of poverty.

I have this nagging fear of being broke, this continuous drive to NOT be broke. This drive sometimes creates an overwhelming focus on my business. When I have an overwhelming focus on business it can create an overwhelming neglect of almost everything else.

This drive creates incredible imbalance in my life. I become selfish with my thoughts and my time. Neglect of my Bride became the unfortunate byproduct of this obsession.

The months leading up to her uttering the word *divorce*, I was in one of my manic, obsessed, only-business-matters, selfish mind-sets.

Stacey has endured many of these episodes in our marriage. But this time was different. She read it differently. She thought I didn't care anymore. That I was uninterested in her and her needs. She began to withdraw her support of me. And I felt it. I took her withdrawal to mean that she was losing interest in me. It made me resent her.

"Why doesn't she support me?" "Why does she spend so much money?" "Why is she so selfish?" "Why don't we have more sexy time?" (OK, I know that's too much information...but I'm trying to paint the true picture of what was going through my mind.)

Our selfish thoughts were driving a wedge between us. We were only looking at the situation through our own lenses. We were not considering for even a second what the other was thinking and feeling.

We didn't resolve things on that trip to Mexico. We staggered on that path until we finally had a "come to Jesus" conversation on January 1, 2013.

On New Year's Eve of 2012 we had a party at the house. Several of our good friends attended. I had this bad feeling the whole night. I was sad, angry, and disheartened most of the night. I tried to keep smiling and keep the "good times" facade up for our guests' sake, but I was hurting inside.

That night after the guests left, Stacey went to bed at around two in the morning. I stayed in the basement to collect my thoughts, arriving in the bedroom at around quarter after three, but I could not sleep. I stared at the ceiling truly considering life without Stacey for the first time.

Without sleeping at all I waited for the first signs of Stacey waking up. When she did I began to pour my heart out to her. She did the same. We talked and cried and talked and cried for a couple of hours. Both realizing that we had not, for a second, considered the other's feelings in all of this.

We made a pact to work first on our marriage (from then on), our communication, and our appreciation for each other…to return to that feeling we both had back in 1998…when we said, "I do!"

It was in that conversation that I came to the realization that I am not driven by success, or riches, or number of homes sold; I'm driven by the fear of poverty, by the obligation to never be broke again. There'll be more on that in upcoming articles. I will get deeply introspective on this topic.

The moral of the story is that even the best marriages (which is what most people around us think we have) need work. They need care. They need open and honest communication…continuously…to survive…to thrive. Too often we get caught up in our own wants, needs, fears, desires, and interpretations…without considering those of our significant others.

We need to appreciate every second we have with that special person. We cannot take any of it or them for granted. We cannot say "I love you" too much. We must always consider how powerful we felt…how joyful it was…how excited we were…when we said, "I do!"

I'm happy to report that Stacey and I are doing fantastic! We have worked on us and will continue to work on us…for what I hope is… forever!

After the holidays, I went back to the office with the same question I had in October of 2000, when I walked along the shores of the Atlantic on the phone with a jackass client trying to keep one lousy deal together, because I had to keep that one lousy deal together. I said once again, "There's got to be a better way!"

So, I set a goal for 2013 to sell 150 homes and work no evenings, no weekends, and no Fridays! I also set the goal to go on ten vacations on top of it!

Stacey rolled her eyes when I told her the goals that I had set. She smiled and said, "That sounds great!" But I could read her expression as, "Yeah right! I'll believe it when I see it!"

To be perfectly open and transparent with you now, I didn't even really believe it myself! However, the vision in my head was clear. I would visualize how it looked and how it felt as I lay in bed at night.

For me to be able to actually operate as the CEO of my business and get out of my own way, I would need better systems and would need to provide more opportunities for my team.

So, in January of 2013, I went on zero appointments. I referred every lead out to team members! In February—zero appointments. I was actually starting to believe that this far-fetched idea and goal was possible.

By the end of the year we sold 151 homes. I went on three appointments. I worked no evenings, no weekends, and no Fridays.

The revolution in my mind-set created a true revolution in my business and more importantly in my life!

Sometimes it takes extreme measures and near catastrophic losses in our live for us to finally wake up and find a better way.

CHAPTER 26

Database Reboot

On November 16, 2013, my Bride Stacey and I sat down on an overstuffed leather sofa on the second floor of the Gaylord Texan Resort in Dallas, Texas.

The time was 8:35 a.m., and we had just eaten breakfast. At breakfast we made a big decision. Our decision was to skip the fourth and final day of the real estate conference we were attending. No, we hadn't decided to play hooky in order to slide down the frozen slide at the Chinese Ice Sculpture exhibit. Our decision wasn't to saunter over to the Glass Cactus Nightclub for some day drinking…no, we decided to spend the entire day organizing, recategorizing, and weeding my database. I know, exciting!

After a couple of failed attempts to log onto the resort's Wi-Fi, I was able to wrangle the password from one of the event staff. The conference apparently had their own private Wi-Fi network set up through the hotel, and now we had access!

We made a successful Internet connection and logged into Top Producer, the CRM program we've used for many years.

During the three days of the real estate conference that we'd attended there were several really good speakers like Jairek Robbins (Tony's son) and Darren Hardy, the CEO of *Success* magazine. On the real estate side of things there wasn't a whole lot of new takeaways for us.

We did, however, have several very successful strategy sessions together over meals and several cocktails. In those sessions, we walked away with three very important objectives that we wanted to implement right away for the business:

1. Clean up the database.
2. Implement and deploy a printed monthly newsletter.
3. Design a plan for ongoing proper communication with our contacts in the database.

Now here's the thing: I got my license in July of 1998 and started practicing full-time in January of 2000. It was now November of 2013, and I had yet to implement a plan for proper communication for my database.

Up until that moment my communication plan consisted of a monthly canned generic letter from Brian Buffini and a yearly refrigerator calendar. And sure, on a rare occasion I would even call a handful of people from the database. Nothing was authentic, and nothing was consistent.

So we started digging into Top Producer with three things in mind:

1. Delete all of the excess contacts that cluttered the hell out of the database. All the old Internet leads, hotlines leads, dead people, etc. In the end we were only left with past clients, current clients, people we knew, vendors, current leads, and real estate agents.

2. Retag everyone that makes it past the first cut. At this point, we had way too many similar and redundant tags. We wanted congruency. Our new tags would be HUG (we got this term from the book Hug Your Customers), Client A, B, and C, SOI A, B, and C, Vendor A, B, and C, and Agent.

3. Determine if anyone in the database had sold their home with another agent since being entered.

Here's a real quick definition of the ABCs (it's easy as 1,2,3…as simple as do re mi…man, I miss Michael Jackson!):

A. People that would definitely do business with you and refer you.
B. People you think will do business with you and refer you.
C. You don't know if these people will do business with you or refer you, but you're going to find out.

The database reboot ended up taking three full days. And I mean three, full, days! I didn't take calls or let my team interrupt me at all during the database cleanse.

Now, I know deep in my gut that I was not doing a good job communicating with my database, but I couldn't have possibly imagined what I found by going through it person-by-person.

To my horrific surprise, we counted thirty-seven people from the database that had sold their home with another agent! We didn't even factor in the number of unconverted leads. We can't even begin to tally the number of buy side deals we missed out on from those thirty-seven sellers. I would imagine at least 60 percent of them purchased another home in my marketplace. Let's do the quick math on these thirty-seven listing deals I missed out on. My average commission check is right around

$5,000. 37 x $5,000 = $185,000! That's $185,000 I missed out on sadly by not doing what can be done very easily! Unearthing this unfortunate lost treasure reiterated our desperate need for a better system for the database communication.

After the database was power-washed and reorganized, we began to outline our proper communication plan.

Here's what we came up with:

- An authentic and honest printed monthly newsletter (strategically crafted to deepen the relationship, provide third-party endorsements, and promote referrals)
- Greeting cards: New Year's, spring, Fourth of July, Thanksgiving, and birthday (a well-crafted message was written for each card, and the entire process was uploaded in SendOutCards.com, which is now handled automatically).
- Year-End Refrigerator Calendar that are big enough to write notes and appointments on. We use MagnetStreet.com for the calendars.

We also outlined a calling schedule based on A, B, and C. As were called every other month. Bs every quarter, and Cs twice yearly.

I haven't made a single call yet. I know it's crazy, a real estate agent that doesn't like to make phone calls, but I want to be as open and honest with you as possible. Making phone calls all the time just isn't something I want to do. When I finally started to run my business like a business in 2010 things changed dramatically.

Then, at the end of 2012 when I wanted to focus more on helping my team by operating as CEO, things changed again for the better.

In 2013, I sold 151 homes working no evenings, no weekends, and no Fridays! But I knew there was so much more we could do if we properly communicated with the database. So, after implementing the communication plan that Stacey and I masterminded during our wine and steak soaked strategy sessions at the Gaylord Texan resort in Dallas, Texas, our business jumped from 151 homes sold in 2013 to 206 in 2014. While still working the same schedule of no evenings, no weekends, and no Fridays… and not making a single cold call or even an outbound call to my database, if I'm being embarrassingly honest with you.

My business model is a bit different than most. My company is just me and my team. That's it. We focus on selling homes and creating great customer experiences. I spend zero time on recruiting agents to my team.

Probably the biggest misnomer of real estate franchises is that they are even in the real estate sales business. They are not. They are in the agent recruiting business (with the hopes that some of the agents actually figure out how to sell some homes). This is not a knock on franchises; it's just my opinion.

So my little team and I ended 2014 with 206 homes sold, and $1,008,000 in commissions with nearly $700,000 of it coming from the database/soi.

To make a long story longer, I strolled into 2015 with only three strategic objectives:

1. Hire Vyral marketing to add PEDs (performance enhancing drugs, for those that don't watch much ESPN) to my database marketing with twice-monthly market update videos.
2. Add continuously to my e-mail list.
3. Add strategically to my newsletter mailing list.

That's it! Those are the only changes.

As I write this on July 8, 2015, we have closed 128 homes and have forty-two pending. Our pace will have us swilling spiked eggnog at just over 250 homes sold for 2015. Not bad for a guy that doesn't make any phone calls.

We are tracking at $1.2 million in commissions with just over $800,000 from the database/SOI.

If you have any questions, or if you want copies of any and or all of the material I send to the database just let me know bart@bartsellshouses.com or visit www.realestategoodlife.com.

CHAPTER 27

Proper Communication

Building a successful real estate business can be accomplished in a number of different ways. However, the ONLY way to build a long-term, eventually sellable, extremely rewarding, dollar productive business is to start with the database/SOI.

One of my many mistakes in this business was to chase *other* things before becoming serious about the database.

In 2004, I went to a Brian Buffini Turning Point Retreat. The event was fantastic, and everything that Brian said made perfect sense. I even hired his company to coach me one-on-one, which they did for the better part of a year. After leaving one-on-one coaching, I continued with his self-paced coaching program, because I really enjoyed getting the package of stuff he sent me each month.

Each package contained audio CDs with a range of inspirational messages and real estate specific tactics. I still listen to those CDs! Also included was a letter to be sent to my database, and two packs of notecards for handwritten notes. Each pack contained twenty-five notecards.

We religiously sent that letter to our database for eight years. So to say I did nothing with the database would be an understatement, but to think that a *canned* letter with a message about how to unclog a sink was *proper communication* is too far of a stretch.

As I discussed in the previous chapter, finally, after over a decade in the business, we sat down and created a specific plan for *proper communication*.

Here's what I know through maniacal tracking and measuring:

- SOI/database delivers a 10 percent transaction conversion
- Internet leads convert at 1.8–2.3 percent
- Expired direct mail/calling converts at 1.2 percent
- Open House leads convert at 1 percent
- FSBO's convert at 0.8 percent

Now, keep in mind that these are my statistics. Your market may be a bit different. However, the overall theme will still apply.

Now as I talk to agents from all over the country I see a recurring theme. They're chasing everything but the database. They spend hundreds and hundreds of dollars a month on Zillow leads and not a dime on the database.

There is a place in your business for any type of marketing and lead generation system that produces a positive ROI (return on investment).

We did all of the above and then some, but we finally got wise enough to spend some dough and have a plan for the database.

Here's specifically what we do:

- Monthly printed newsletter to everyone tagged HUG in the database
- Greeting cards for: New Year's, spring, Fourth of July, Thanksgiving, and birthday for all tagged as HUG.
- Yearly calendar with an authentic and appreciative letter around Christmas time for all HUGs.
- Video e-mails to our e-mail database twice a month.

The people tagged HUG in our database are past clients, current clients, SOI A+'s, SOI A's, our favorite vendors, and strategics.

The strategics are people like the Mayor of Valparaiso, some of the local business owners that I admire, school superintendents and principals, and positive people with large networks in the community.

The e-mail database is everyone we have an e-mail for! Right now the list is around 8,000.

You'll see in the upcoming chapter, "The Eighteen Steps to an Extra Million Dollars," that adding people consistently to the database is one of the most essential aspects of building a lucrative and, more importantly, rewarding real estate business.

If Internet leads convert at 2 percent and the database at 10 percent, how can I possibly justify spending more on Internet leads? I CAN'T!

Please don't make the same mistakes I have! Start immediately with consistently adding to the database while properly communicating with it.

Here's what I would also suggest to you. Call them. Consistently.

Call A+s every single month.
Call As no less than every other month.
Call Bs at least once a quarter.
Call Cs no less than twice a year.

In the previous chapter I defined As, Bs, and Cs. What I didn't define was the A+, which is simply someone you like that sends you at least one referral each and every year.

I'll be honest with you, as I always am. I do not call my database. This is not recommended. It's one of the many things I still do wrong. My goal is to hire someone to do it for me. I do not like to call people, and that includes my database. It's sad but true. I tried to fight it for many years. It being the dislike of calling people. I couldn't warm to it; it was too unnatural for me. It didn't make me feel good. So I built a business that doesn't require me to call anyone! Boo yeah!

If my math is true, then let's look at the power of the database.

There are currently nine-hundred people on my monthly newsletter list. The math says that with proper communication, I'll enjoy a 10 percent transaction return, whether a direct deal or referral.

900 x 10% = 90 Transactions. My average commission is $5,000. 90 x $5,000 = $450,000.

We spend about $1.10 per newsletter x 900 = $		= $990
We spend $.50 per notecard x 5 x 900		= $2,250
We spend around $1500 on the calendars		= $1,500
Vyral Marketing runs me $6,000 per year		= $6,600

That's a total investment of $11,340.

Here's the best part. We're in our first full year with Vyral Marketing. Therefore my tracking numbers are still being tabulated.

Vyral Marketing is the company that helps me create the two videos sent to the e-mail database every month. Vyral edits the videos, adds cool effects, and then sends out all of the e-mails from their servers. I've been over-the-moon happy with their company!

Back to the math. So if I invested $11,340 and got back $450,000, I'd be pretty stoked, right?

Here's why I continue to be more and more excited about spending time with and investing in the database…

This year we aren't tracking at $450,000 as the math would suggest from the database. We're tracking at ending the year with $800,000 earned directly from the database!

My 10 percent transaction return theory was established before hiring Vyral Marketing to add an even more substantial layer of communication to the database.

However, before the final numbers do come in, let's use the 10 percent already proven statistic to run an exciting scenario for you. Let's say you have 150 in your SOI/database. Statistically that's how many people the average adult American knows.

Let's also assume you are not properly communicating to your database. It's probably a safe assumption.

Let's also assume that you'll implement one of the most important steps of the Eighteen Steps to a Million and add two people each week to your database. And we'll even round down and say you'll add a hundred people a year.

Let's also say your average commission is $5,000 per transaction.

Year One: 150 People in database 10% Return 15 Transactions x $5,000 = $75,000
Year Two: 250 People in database 10% Return 25 Transactions x $5,000 = $125,000
Year Three: 350 People in database 10% Return 35 Transactions x $5,000 = $175,000
Year Four: 450 People in database 10% Return 45 Transactions x $5,000 = $225,000
Year Five: 550 People in database 10% Return 55 Transactions x $5,000 = $275,000

That's $875,000 EXTRA dollars produced directly from the database!

This does not include all the extra buyers created due to all the extra listings you'll be taking. This does not include all the extra people added to the database from the direct referrals created because of your *proper communication*.

Now you can see why I get so excited about this stuff! It's how I can make the wild claim of "The Eighteen Steps to an Extra Million Dollars!"

What a great business we are in!

Please do not disregard this information because you need a quick fix from an Internet buyer. Do not disregard this information because the database takes time to see results.

DO THIS STUFF IMMEDIATELY...because it works—GUARANTEED!

CHAPTER 28

Time Management and Bologna Sandwiches

I got home from work and was starving. My preload shift at UPS usually had me home by ten each morning. I stormed into the kitchen and prepared an exquisite gourmet meal. Two fried bologna sandwiches consisting of simply four pieces of Oscar Mayer all-beef bologna fried nearly to a crisp and four pieces of Butternut wheat bread.

In the living room directly in front of the La-Z-Boy, a beat-up wooden TV tray desperately waited for the meal to arrive. Lying next to the recliner was Abigail, my roommate's beautiful Rottweiler.

The year was 1993, and I was sharing an apartment on the corner of Washington and 23rd in Chesterton, Indiana. Both of my roommates, Joe Garavalia and Jerry Splitgerber, worked construction Monday through Friday from around seven in the morning till three in the afternoon. So Abigail and I always had the place to ourselves when I got home from UPS.

I placed the paper plate loaded with delicious sandwiches on the TV tray and frolicked back into the kitchen for a cold beverage to wash it all down.

Upon my return, a horrific scene filled my now grief-stricken eyes! Only one beautiful sandwich remained on the plate. The other defenseless all-beef bologna, my lovingly prepared sandwich, was being murdered before my very eyes by the once sweet and innocent Abigail!

"Abigail! No!" I screamed. But it was too late. The victim was gone and not a breadcrumb of evidence remained.

I learned a valuable lesson that day. "You can't trust a dog to guard your food!"

And while we're on the subject of trust…you should never trust anyone with your time.

We all have the same amount of it: 24 hours, 1,440 minutes, and 86,400 seconds in each day. And yet there are agents out there that sell hundreds of home a year, while most struggle to sell eight to ten.

In our business, time is the most precious commodity and yet it is also the most blatantly wasted, abused, destroyed, and disrespected one. A lot of the time (no pun intended) the perpetrator is you.

You know what I'm talking about. You stroll into the office at 10:20 a.m., fire up the computer, scroll through dozens of pointless e-mails, then click around on Facebook, make a few comments, like even more. Then Billy stumbles by from two cubicles down and begins to bend your ear about his only pending that is now on the ropes because his buyer charged twelve hundred dollars' worth of furniture from IKEA.

Oh darn, look at the time…who's hungry for lunch? Two hours later you're back in the office just in time to check more e-mails!

We must make a pact to guard our time, even from ourselves.

If a masked marauder donkey kicked your front door open, stormed in, and started after your prized possessions like your enormous television, one of your iPads, or, God forbid, your iPhone…you'd put up a helluva fight! And these are all easily replaceable possessions.

Time is not replaceable, sadly…not at all. So, Katy, bar the doors to your time! Keep it guarded!

Time is what we want most, but what we use worst.
—WILLIAM PENN

CHAPTER 29

Newsletters

L et me take time right now to reiterate a very important point that I've already covered—just to make sure you get the full impact of the profound improvement it had on my business.

The topic I want to cover is the newsletter. I know it's an out of date concept according to many. My experience with it has forever changed my business. More importantly, it has provided a leveraged means of building deep rapport on a one-to-many basis.

The idea is simple. Write authentic articles. Share what's going on in your life. Make only 20–25 percent of the newsletter about real estate. People would much rather hear about you and your interesting stories than about boring interest rates.

My accountant, attorney, and financial advisor all send me a monthly or quarterly newsletter. They all stink! Because it's all *canned* boring industry-specific stuff.

Please take the time to build out a printed monthly newsletter for your business. Do not let anything hold you back. Once the template is designed the rest is just swipe and deploy. You can even have my template if you'd like. You know where to find it: www.realestategoodlife.com.

The year prior to deploying the newsletter we sold 151 homes. Not too bad, right? The following year we sold 206 homes. And our commissions from SOI/database went from $362,360 to $671,539!

Take a look at this breakdown:

Year	Total Commission	Commission from SOI	Homes Sold
2013	$742,250	$362,360	151
2014	$1,008,000	$671,539	206
2015	$1,200,000	$800,000	250 **

**2015 is not over yet. We are tracking at the numbers listed.

In this chapter, I want to include some examples of main articles I've written for the newsletter. If you'd like to copy any of them, feel free. I want to give you an idea of what I mean by authentic and heartfelt. I know what I just said was a bit counterintuitive (copy if you want…and be authentic)…but you know what I mean!

Here are some example Main Articles I've written for my newsletter:

The Pursuit of Happiness

Soon we will celebrate another holiday, Independence Day, most commonly referred to as the Fourth of July.

My two favorite holidays, aside from Christmas, are Thanksgiving and Independence Day.

Both remind me of the blessing we each have that most others do not. We are free, we are able, and we have the right to pursue happiness. Most of the world does not! It seems to me that these unalienable rights are all too often overlooked.

This nation is becoming more and more cynical and weak, lazy, and unappreciative of the "luck" we all share.

Eight years ago, Stacey and I gave up watching the news and reading newspapers. Why? Because both were filled with garbage. The news, if believed, delivers the message that we live in the worst "times" of all time. That people are getting more violent, the economy is horrible, and the world is about to run out of every natural resource.

The truth is, crime is down by 50 percent from its peak in the early 1970s, we have the largest economy in the world, still twice that of China (and China has five times as many people), and just two years ago, the second largest oil discovery in the history of the world was made in Texas!

So, when I tell people that we gave up "bad news," I get a lot of rolled eyes. I prefer good news over bad…and years ago, I discovered that I can make my own good news…by pursuing freedom and happiness.

If you can't be happy in this country…then you're likely out of luck. I don't think I've ever heard anyone say, "If I can just make it into Mexico…"

We live in the "land of opportunity," but most of our citizens cannot see the forest through the trees. A foreigner entering the United States is four times more likely to become a millionaire than the very people already living under the blanket of opportunity!

Other countries have a visa lottery whereby people enter to "win" a chance to enter this country with a work visa—a "chance" to come here and work! We have a growing portion of this population that is doing everything possible NOT to work.

> *Freedom has its life in the hearts, the actions, the spirit of*
> *men and so it must be daily earned and refreshed—else like*
> *a flower cut from its life-giving roots, it will wither and die.*
> —DWIGHT D. EISENHOWER

This quote means a lot to me, and it should for everyone. We live in the greatest country, in the greatest of times…and this needs to be celebrated!

This nation was knit together against a common enemy. It was built by shared values, such as freedom, opportunity, and individual rights, but to take advantage of this you MUST also couple those values with ambition, initiative, and self-reliance!

Sure, it was and is an imperfect Union, but we must remember what got us here…united in being about "something." An American ideal developed that made this nation the freest, most innovative, and most opportunity available of any on earth.

So, as you celebrate this upcoming holiday, enjoying the burgers, hot-dogs, and cold drinks…keep in mind WHY.

Take advantage of your opportunity, take advantage of your freedom, and take advantage of your advantage.

We are one nation under God, indivisible, with liberty and justice for all!

I think it's time for us to recommit to our pledges, values, and ideals… that created the very greatness that we daily enjoy, but often daily overlook.

Together we stand in the pursuit of happiness!

Hug someone, kiss someone, salute the flag…and celebrate with the conviction of those that got us here!

We are living on the greatest planet, in the greatest country, during the greatest of times!

God bless you, and God bless the United States of America!

YOLO: You only live once!
What if you only live once?

What if you were only given one time around on this earth, and life truly was short?

Would you do anything differently from what you are doing right now?

I know the answer, you know the answer…so what are you waiting for?

Right now, as you read this article:

Are you living the life of your dreams?
Are you in the relationship that you deserve?
Do you have enough money?
Are you in the physical shape that you want to be in?
Are you looking forward to going to work today, or are you dreading it?
Are you achieving greatness in your life?

Recently I woke up and realized that I was not doing everything I could be doing to live the life that I desire and deserve.

In that stream of consciousness I searched for "what" it was I was looking for, and what I determined…was greatness.

I owe it to myself, my family, my friends, and God…to pursue greatness—not greatness as defined by society, or anyone else for that matter, but greatness as it is defined by me.

You and I will now pursue greatness together!

Before you roll your eyes, crumble this newsletter up, or rip it to shreds, hear me out! Please accept that your definition of greatness lies within. It cannot be determined by anyone other than you! Do NOT let external factors determine your definition. Your greatness MUST be authentic!

There are three primary reasons why people do not reach greatness in their life:

1. They have no idea what greatness looks like.
2. They know what greatness looks like, but they have no idea how to get there.
3. They know what greatness looks like, and they know how to get there…but they've never held themselves (or allowed others to hold them) to a high enough standard of achievement long enough, or consistently enough, to achieve greatness.

Here's the part that you must embrace: we were all born with greatness inside. We were not destined for mediocrity. We were designed for greatness. There isn't a single person that, deep down, has the intentional thought of, "You know, this week I'm going to go to work and produce a fraction of what I am actually capable of. I'm going to go home tonight and give my wife 12 percent of the love and attention she deserves. This weekend I'm going to spend a fragment of the quality time I'm capable of with my kids." Nobody thinks that way, but most act that way.

What I want to share with you is common sense, but not common practice.

Recently I started a real estate agent mastermind group. The reason was simple: to help real estate agents reach greatness in their business. The more important reason: to reach greatness for myself.

A few years ago I created a Greatness List (my version of a bucket list). As we move along in these articles, I will share the items on the list. For now, I'll give you a few that I've accomplished.

1. Quit tobacco: for twenty-eight years I used smokeless tobacco (Skoal). In June of 2014, I quit cold turkey and have not looked back.
2. Get straight teeth: when I was in the seventh grade my mother wanted me to get braces. Having witnessed what my older brother Larry went through, I said no thanks. I've regretted it ever since. In November of 2011 I got braces, and in September of 2014 they came off! Thanks Dr. Brenda! (Best orthodontist in the world by the way!)
3. Learn to swim: yep, never learned to swim as a kid. Friends and family thought I was afraid of the water. Nope, just afraid of drowning! Self-taught in my backyard 2012.
4. Write and publish a book. Wayne Dyer says "don't die with the music inside." When I started in real estate I had very little guidance and learned the hard way. I vowed that once I became successful I would show others exactly how I did it! My plan is to write and publish multiple books within my genre of expertise, real estate.

This article will be a multipart series, so this is just the teaser. Please understand as you read the articles that this is not about regretting things in your past. It's about circumventing regret in your future. I understand that most all people will do absolutely nothing different—and will later regret it. But what if you did the opposite?

What if you did what most all people in this country DON'T do? And that is to define what greatness is for you—and then GO FOR IT!

Part 2 coming next month.

YOLO Part 2:

This is Part 2 of our journey together, our journey to greatness.

We were born to move forward, to climb, to improve. We were meant to stretch and grow and push ourselves toward a better and more fulfilling life. We were designed to pursue and live the life of our dreams.

But somewhere along the way, we stopped dreaming! We stopped reaching. We stopped pursuing. And it's not ALL our fault!

Our parents wanted to protect us so they told us to be "realistic." Our teachers and schools followed the curriculum given to them, and not knowing any better they taught us to be average. They taught us to be workers. Our universities train us to get a job. Our media brainwashes us to spend all of our money, the money that our parents never talked about, the money that our schools never taught us about.

So most ALL people become trapped in overwhelmingly average, mediocre, stagnant, and increasingly disappointing lives.

They've stopped taking risks (maybe never did) and followed the herd to mediocrity. They've settled for jobs that lead nowhere, for relationships that sink spirits, and they've established habits that hold them back, habits that are self-destructive.

It's no wonder that so many people suffer from anxiety, endure midlife crises—you would too, if you woke up one morning and realized you were nowhere near the life you always dreamed about, the life you were meant to live.

Maybe we're talking about you, and today is the day you "woke up!"

Let's conduct a progress report on your life right now!

I want you to look at your life and answer these simple, yet chillingly profound, questions:

1. Am I closer to living the life of my dreams this year than I was last year?
2. Have I been getting ahead in life, standing still, or falling behind?
3. Do I even have a definition of what greatness is for my life?
4. Am I truly moving forward toward greatness and the life of my dreams? Or am I waiting for "the right time?"

Again, please only define greatness and the life of your dreams yourself. It is not defined by society or anyone else for that matter. It MUST be defined by you!

Here's a scary thought, maybe you have no idea what greatness (for you) looks like. Maybe you've never defined the life of your dreams.

In my favorite book, *Think and Grow Rich* by Napoleon Hill, Napoleon talks about definiteness of purpose.

After you answer the four questions above, you must also determine your definiteness of purpose. You cannot get "there" if you don't know where there is!

If you don't know where you are going, any road will get you there.

You are in full control of your destiny, but only when you have reached clarity regarding what that is.

Please determine IMMEDIATELY what *that* is!

YOLO: Part 3

You only live once.

In Part 1 I asked you a tough question: "Are you currently living the life of your dreams?" You answered no.

You and I also discussed greatness. Your greatness. Not greatness as defined by society, the media, or anyone other than you...your greatness.

We also went through the three reasons why people aren't great: They don't know what greatness looks like. Or, they know what it looks like but have no idea how to get there. Or, they know what it looks like and know how to get there, but have never held themselves to a high enough standard long enough to experience the awesomeness of greatness.

We determined that number three was your reason why.

In Part 2, we looked at definiteness of purpose, which means that you need to have a clearly defined idea of what "it" looks like, "it" being—your Greatness—your Freedom—your Happiness.

Now in Part 3 I will touch on a subject and idea that I'm a little nervous about. I'm nervous because I already know the answer to the question. But I'm not sure if you are authentic enough to answer it honestly.

In January of 2014, when I published my very first Good Life newsletter, I described being transparent and authentic to you. I also stated that I wanted to have conversations that most people are not comfortable having. In doing so, in today's mamby pamby society the risk is "offending" someone. In order to deliver authentic content and articles to you, I have to be thick skinned enough to not care about offending those that at the end of the day are easily offended.

So, here we go…

> *All of the animals except man know that the*
> *principal business of life is to enjoy it.*
> —SAMUEL BUTLER

We all know that our life's purpose is much more than a job, more than a "career," and certainly more than a paycheck. A life of meaning is not limited to a life of financial means.

Yet many of us suffer the self-imposed misery of doing unfulfilling work simply to make ends meet. We take jobs and work jobs that we don't love—most don't even like them—for no better reason than to make a living.

If you are going to spend the best hours of the best years of your life working, how can you possibly justify doing something that you do not like?

In this society, there are very few "have-tos." We all work because we "have to." But why? Why do we have to?

"Well Bart, because I have bills and responsibilities—that's why?"

But why do you have the bills you have? Most of them are not out of necessity, are they? The situation we find ourselves in is always self-imposed. It's always because of our own doing. The choices we make create our situation.

I remember when Stacey and I were first married. We had a house payment, one car payment, utilities, food, and insurance. Our total cost of living was $1,821 a month. Now it's just over $10,000 a month and we don't have any car payments or credit card debt.

Our cost of living didn't just happen! We created it with the choices we've made. Now don't get me wrong, we live a better life than most people. A lot of our expenses are created by the number of vacations we go on, the entertaining we do, and the entertainment we enjoy.

But that $10,000 monthly BILL is self-imposed.

If I were stuck working at the rock quarry or the coal mines to pay for that living I would be miserable. I'm fortunate enough to look forward to going into the office each day. Now, I'm not saying that I don't deal with stressful situations, uncomfortable conversations, and disappointments…I do. But through trial and error, making mistakes, taking risks, and getting out of my comfort zone, I actually enjoy what I do for a living!

I'm not done yet. What I "do" for a living doesn't fulfill all of my need for purpose. I am currently building another outlet from within my business. I will be helping real estate agents duplicate the system I built called "The Real Estate Good Life." I will be giving them marketing ideas, systems, and processes, and much more.

Giving. It's a higher purpose for me, because it's not about me. My ultimate purpose is to help others realize their greatness. It's taken me a long time to figure out that my purpose wasn't about me.

I know I'm rambling, but my point is simple but not easy. It's counterintuitive to what most all American adults actually do with their lives when it comes to work.

You can choose to do anything you want with your time. I ask you: Is what you are *choosing* to do with it currently something you enjoy? Do you get up each day energized and excited about going to work? Do you get lost in your work often? Does time seem to get away from you when you are completely immersed in something that you truly enjoy?

If you cannot answer with a resounding "YES!" to these questions, then you know it's time for a change.

Let me give you a quick example and an anomaly. My nephew Brandon Vickrey is a junior at Valparaiso University. He is a journalism and communication major. He decided long ago that he wanted to be a sports broadcaster and sports journalist. He spent his high school years calling games, writing about games, was the editor of the school newspaper, and the sports anchor of the school's morning announcements television show.

Brandon has spent the past two summers as the play-by-play announcer for the Whiting Oilmen baseball team, and he is currently the team's Director of Communications. He also is a sports writer for the Post Tribune, and the play-by-play voice for the Valparaiso University Lady Crusaders basketball team.

While most kids his age are wasting their parents' money on an education they'll never use, playing video games, or boozing it up at frat parties, Brandon is working—not because he has to, but because he loves it!

Thinking about these things in the bigger picture of your life is not something we are taught to do.

This is difficult and something most people NEVER do, but it's time you ask yourself a question you likely have been avoiding for too long: "Is what I'm doing to make a living really what I want to be doing?"

This is a tough question for most people, because they don't know what they want to be doing (need to establish definiteness of purpose). Worse yet, they have stopped actively looking—yikes! They've settled into a *job* and have accepted it as their fate.

Listen, I know that most everyone that reads this article will do nothing about their current situation. I'm not a delusional optimist! But maybe it will hit home for you, and YOU will Decide to Live the Life of *Your* Dreams.

Thanks for reading! Next month we will find out if you are being authentic! You are either truly being yourself, or you are NOT! Dun Dun Da! (Those last three words are to be read as dramatic and suspenseful sounds!)

Spenders or Savers?

My financial advisor said something very unsettling the other day. She said, "My job keeps getting harder and harder…you wouldn't believe HOW HARD it is to get anyone under the age of 50 to save and invest money!"

Unfortunately this comes as no surprise.

I've mentioned to you before that happiness is my number one goal in life. And when I picture happiness, I see a pyramid. Happiness is the pyramid, and the three sides are made up of health, wealth, and freedom.

From my vantage point, we've allowed ourselves to be duped into living paycheck to paycheck. We've been lured into consumerism!

If you pay close attention to television commercials you will realize that most all things being advertised are NOT needed. But the selling of these "things" are designed to stir your emotions.

The new car makes you feel successful.
The skinny jeans make you feel sexy.
The Rolex watch makes you feel rich.

In this country it seems we are addicted to spending! Saving rates have plummeted starting in the mideighties. The average saving rate from the caveman until around 1985 was 10 percent. Meaning that for every one hundred dollars earned you saved ten dollars.

The all-time low was in 2005 when it hit a num-skull-ing (sometimes I make up words, lol!) low of 0.8 percent. So for every one hundred dollars earned, the average American was saving eighty CENTS! Keep in mind that is a very skewed number. It is weighted and counterbalanced by the savers. Savers will typically always save. With that in mind, that means the "average" American was spending more than they made and saving zero, zilch, nada!

The average American between the ages of twenty-five and thirty-five has a net worth of $10,400. That plus a firm handshake can buy them a decent shed to store all of the worthless things they've wasted all their money on!

Now, don't get me wrong, I'm not preaching from the soap box. I've made plenty of money mistakes over the years. When I was dead broke, what drove me to work so hard was MONEY. Once I started making money—I started spending money, lots of it!

In 2002 Stacey and I had accumulated $32,000 in credit card debt! We worked hard and paid it all off. We thought we had learned our lesson, but not so fast! In 2008 I opened a credit card statement and the balance was $38,000! What the heck happened?

The real estate market was tanking, and apparently I was subsidizing an overzealous business budget with my credit card. And in some ways, Stacey and I had justified it as "business" expenses. But the stressful reality was that it was my name on that credit card statement, not my business!

So once again we hunkered down and paid it off. We have not had a credit card balance since!

It was after paying off that large credit card balance that I really, for the first time, started thinking about becoming debt free.

I remember my grandfather telling me when I was younger that he once bought a washing machine, "…on credit back in 1943…and I'm still paying for it!" he would say.

For me, I've decided that debt cannot exist in my pursuit of happiness plan. Debt denies freedom. Debt creates stress. Stress undermines health. Debt subtracts from wealth.

If my formula is Happiness = Health, Wealth, and Freedom…then debt MUST be eradicated!

Currently, we're still spending too much. But we're working on it, right, Honey? Honey? (Crickets.)

Anyway, we are saving for retirement, saving for college, investing for wealth, donating to charities, and aggressively paying off our house. We have no credit card debt, no car payments, and are scheduled to have our house paid off by December 31, 2016!

Listen. If I can do this, anyone can!

The first step is to always look around, and then do the *exact opposite* of what everyone else is doing.

If most of America has become a nation of undisciplined spenders and consumers, do the opposite! If your neighbors' unfettered spending and material extravagance is writing his obituary in the ink of stress, do the opposite!

Side note: you want to become a Debt Free Millionaire?

Read these six books: *Think and Grow Rich, The Millionaire Next Door, Rich Dad Poor Dad, The Richest Man in Babylon, Your Money or Your Life* (the 1993 or older versions), and *Total Money Makeover*.

Now we all know money doesn't buy happiness, but it can buy freedom. Money misused, however, can buy servitude, bondage, and slavery. If you have to "make" money to service your debt created by your things, you cannot be free.

Wealth and happiness can be interchangeable, but only if your definition of wealth hasn't been corrupted by society's definition of wealth. Society says that wealth is stuff, and because of this definition the bridge between wealth and happiness collapses.

My definition of wealth has changed drastically over the course of the past ten years. Maybe, just maybe, I'm maturing. My definition of wealth is having enough money so that I don't have to answer to anyone else.

My definition of wealth is having an opportunity to help and witness in the development of my children. To be "there" for them and not always at work…working for things.

So maybe my definition is a little counterintuitive to that of society's… If that's true, then maybe I'm on to something!

The course of my writing veered and swerved a little in this article but I know you get the point I am trying to make. When I write these articles I typically just sit down and write them straight through…shooting from the hip with the ever present goal of keeping your attention and maybe even entertaining you along the way.

Have a great day and for God's sake—wage a war on debt and start SAVING some money!

Advice for My Twenty-One-Year-Old Son (He's Seven Now).

It was Sunday, May 24, 2015 at 10:06 a.m. Deuce (my seven-year-old son Bart II) and I were in the car together driving to Gordman's. Gordman's is a retail store in Valparaiso over by the Cinemark Theatre that has a menagerie of goods for sale at relatively cheap prices.

We were going on this day to check out the toys. Out of the blue Deuce said, "Dad, I wish people could live forever!"

Me, "That would be awesome!"

Deuce then dropped some profound conjecture on me, "What would also be cool is if you could pick an age and stay that age for as long as you wanted!"

So of course I asked, "What age would you choose?"

He said, "Twenty-one."

Me: "Why twenty-one?"

Seven-year-old Deuce: "Because when you're twenty-one you can do whatever you want. You can join the army, you can shoot guns, and you can drink beer! You know, you can shoot guns and drink beer with your army buddies!" I laughed, of course, and then we proceeded to Gordman's where we bought two boomerangs, a really cool water balloon making system, and a pack of four army guys that goes with a set he's been playing with lately.

Later that day I was telling Stacey the story of what Deuce said, and it really got me thinking. What would I want Deuce to know at age twenty-one that would have the most positive impact on his life. So I started making some notes.

Here's what I have so far:

1. Eat right most of the time.
2. Exercise regularly.
3. Drink in moderation. (Hopefully soon I will heed my own advice!)
4. No tobacco.
5. No drugs, and that includes prescription drugs like mood enhancers, sleep aids, etc. Well maybe you can take the little blue bill if you ever need it; it probably won't hurt you...but it's *hard* to tell, lol.
6. Never fight but always defend.
7. Always dance. Deuce, let me tell you my secret to picking up chicks back in the day: hang around guys that are better looking than you—and always dance.
8. Be true to yourself: Follow your heart, set goals that are your goals. Be that kid who saw me in the front row of your first-grade play the other morning who ran up and yelled "Daddy!" and gave me a big hug. Never stop being that kid!
9. Be there: Let go of the past, and don't worry about the future. Live in the now! You know how I make you and your sisters stop and huddle up whenever we're on vacation? When I say, "Hey guys,

look around and take it all in. This will be the only time in your life that we are at the Grand Canyon when Deuce is seven, Maya is twelve, and Madison is fifteen. Remember this moment!" You guys roll your eyes, but you'll thank me one day.

10. Love unconditionally. This one is a little deep, but your future wife will thank you for it. Love people without reservation. Do and say things to and for people out of pure love for them without any strings attached. Let go of any emotion tied to reciprocity or acknowledgement.

11. Give more than you take. You will find that what comes around goes around, and karma is truly a bitch. With that in mind, you always get more when you give more. Help enough people get what they want, and you will always get what you want!

12. No regrets. This does not mean to live recklessly or carelessly. What I'm trying to say is that if you have any inkling to do or try something…just do it!

13. Create your own political party. Today's politics would have our forefathers rolling in their graves. There is a monopoly held by only two parties, and both are broken. Establish your own views, and what you'll find is we need to overhaul the entire system!

14. Don't believe what really religious people tell you. They are innocent victims of their environmental programming. They don't know any better…so don't bother arguing with them. Do your own religious and spiritual research. Check out all of the religions, especially Buddhism.

15. Don't watch the news or read the newspapers.

16. Don't listen to the maniacal puppeteer in your head. Deuce, listen carefully, because I'm about to drop a bombshell! That constant, continuous, manipulative, nagging, fearful, angry, sadistic, masochistic voice that is running its mouth inside your head is NOT YOU! You will think it is. Everyone thinks it is! I thought

it was up until around the time I turned forty-four (last month)! That voice is a looped recording of the programming that you've had in your life. That voice is developed out of our original lizard brain that was designed first and foremost to keep us alive. As soon as you recognize and surrender to the mind-blowing idea that "the voice" is NOT actually you, your life will immediately change forever!

17. Read a lot! Never stop reading. Self-education is one-hundred-fold more powerful than formal education. Work hard at your job, and you will make a living; work hard on yourself, and you'll make a fortune!

18. Vacation often. You may think its normal the amount of times we go on family vacations. But I can assure you, it's not! Most people, most families, don't vacation enough.

19. Get married. Don't let your buddies tell you otherwise. One of the single greatest things you can do is find a great person to marry. Your mother gives me great power. She always has my back, and she is witness to my everyday struggle and greatness.

20. Have kids. You know I gotta tell you buddy, you almost were never born! The reason is that your mother and I thought we were done after two kids. Then one day Stacey says to me, "You want to try for a boy?" I tell her, "I'll have as many kids as you want!" Then voila, nine months later your big head popped out!

21. Talk with friends. This one, I am not very good at...yet. Having close friends and family that you can talk to and be real with is priceless.

22. Don't fart near an open flame. I threw that one in to make sure you were still reading this. And I know you like to talk about farts, so it's a win/win.

23. Step out of your comfort zone. This is one of the surefire ways to cut down on regrets.

24. Hug people. What I love to see when you're around your friends is that you hug them. Boys and girls, it doesn't matter, you're hugging. Don't ever stop hugging. It's scientifically proven that people who hug have less stress in their lives.

25. Root for everyone. What you will sadly realize is that there are a lot of people out there that actually root for people to fail. I've never understood this mind-set. The world is filled with abundance, son. Root for everyone!

26. Do the opposite. Look around and you will see most all people are doing mostly all the same things. Do the opposite.

27. "Things" are overrated. Did you know that just a few years ago your Dad had a BMW, a Corvette Convertible, and a second home in southwest Florida? Sounds great doesn't it? Well, it wasn't. Those things only added temporary and fleeting joy to my life. If fact, they felt more like a lead vest of worry. Don't let anyone ever tell you otherwise; things are overrated!

28. Save money.

29. Forgive: forgiveness is giving up the idea that the past could somehow be different.

30. Be grateful. Every day when you get up think of three things/people that you are grateful for. Do the same when you go to bed each night.

31. Understand that the only normal people you know are the ones that you don't know very well. Think about that one for a second!

32. Keep in mind that the person who is talking about me to you today will be the same person talking about you to me tomorrow.

33. The hardest thing to open is a closed mind, so don't bother.

34. Smile, at everyone.

35. Be nice to the waitress.

36. Be on time.
37. Say please and thank you.
38. Get really good at something.
39. Laugh…a lot!
40. Open doors.
41. Wave at your neighbors.
42. Buy used cars only, and always pay cash.
43. Never hit a woman, ever.
44. Rub some dirt on it.
45. Walk it off.
46. Do not pee into the wind.
47. Don't lie. You'll never have to remember what you said.
48. Don't tell the truth if it's going to hurt someone's feelings.
49. Never say, "Hold my beer. Hey guys…watch this!"
50. Read to your kids every night (until they beg you not to).

OK, I'm out of breath! So that's it for now. If you have any suggestions for me to add to this list, please e-mail me at bart@bartsellshouses.com.

Hope you enjoyed the articles. As you know by now through reading this book and having just read some of my newsletter articles, I'm not a great writer. But I'm making an effort. I'm getting a little better each time I sit down to write. The same will be true for you.

Now go write something and get your newsletter out there!

P.S. After sending out the newsletter that contained the article you just read, I had three requests from people asking to be removed from the mailing list, each of them because of number fourteen on the list!

At first I was upset, but then I realized that in order to be truly authentic, I'm going to have to expect criticism. With that being said, I'm trying to wrap my mind around just writing for an audience of one, doing my best, and then letting go of the result. For it is the worry of the result that keeps most people from ever accessing their inner artist.

CHAPTER 30

Vyral Marketing

As you know, in 2013 I decided to turn my attention to my team. Instead of focusing on myself and my appointments and everything in my head and world, I made a radical change to enhance the lives of those around me without expecting anything in return.

Not that I didn't anticipate anything in return. I'm no Gandhi or Mother Theresa (although that'd be awesome). Everything I'd ever learned pointed me to living by the Golden Rule and that when you give you get.

It was difficult to do as I'd spent my entire career relying on my own hard work and sweat, reaping my own harvest. My team reacted as I only could have hoped. They rose to the occasion and proved that it wasn't just me that could do it.

The mind-set that I had developed over the years was that nobody could do it as well as I could. We work in a business that practically demands that mind-set from us.

The relief in knowing that it doesn't always have to be you is life changing.

You may be thinking, "But Bart, I don't want to build a team." That's fine, but I would strongly suggest you reconsider. The job of being a real estate agent kind of stinks overall. The business of real estate, however, is awesome!

Even if you just employed the basic form of leverage by utilizing virtual assistants, you'd be building somewhat of an actual business. Call up Steve Kantor over at Best Agent Business and discuss it with him. Just don't convince yourself that you're the only one that can do it! That mind-set very well may keep you imprisoned forever.

So the unthinkable happened in 2013, and my team and I sold 151 homes with my schedule of no evenings, no weekends, and no Fridays.

We reorganized the database, outlined the plan for proper communication, and deployed the printed monthly newsletter in 2014. We jumped to 206 homes sold. I would give almost all of the credit to the newsletter and the team.

We entered 2015 with only one real change, and that was hiring Vyral Marketing to add another layer of communication to the database.

I've already described to you what Vyral does, which is to handle almost every aspect of sending two videos per month to my e-mail database.

I'd like to share with you some of the results. Keep in mind that I get nothing for this, no kickback, no sponsorship money, no referral fee. I'm telling you this because it works!

Along with the bi-monthly videos, Vyral also sends specific lead generation e-mails to my database a few times a year. On January 12, 2015, just a few weeks after I hired them, Vyral sent a seller lead generation e-mail to my database that produced:

- 72 Leads
- 13 Listings
- $33,742 in directly attributable commissions

As I write this on September 2, 2015, we've had fifteen closings and $77,615 specifically tracked from Vyral Marketing generated leads, and we are tracking to end the year at just over $100,000 in commissions just from our Vyral Marketing platform.

If you'd like a copy of the exact e-mail that Vyral sent out for me in January, you can grab it at www.realestategoodlife.com.

Now you see why I had to add this extra chapter touting my experience with Vyral. They have been top notch to work with. Frank Klesitz, their CEO, is not only a visionary…more importantly, he's a great guy!

If you'd like see the types of videos that Vyral sends out for me go to www.nwihomesite.com and then click on the Blog link. The direct link is www.nwihomesite.com/blog.

Don't blame Vyral for some of the ridiculous ones! They send me a ton of great content and suggestions for videos. But often I do whatever comes to me in the spur of the moment!

CHAPTER 31

The Inspiration

On May 14, 2015 I was interviewed live on a Google Hangout. The show is called "Keeping It Real" and is hosted by Jeff Manson and Frank Klesitz.

I was so nervous leading up to the interview. Here's some of the thoughts that were going through my head:

"Hope I don't blow it!"

"Why would anyone want to hear what I have to say?"

"I hate my voice!"

"I have a face for radio!"

The show was scheduled to go on live at 6:00 p.m. Central Time (my time). Me, Frank, and Jeff had agreed to get on early at five thirty to talk strategy.

As the time approached, I was literally pacing the office.

"Why did I agree to this?"

"What if I just don't show up and tell them I had an emergency?"

As soon as we all got on the Hangout, my nerves leveled out. I remembered having a preinterview call with Jeff a couple of weeks before the live show. Stacey and I were at Dan Kennedy's Super Conference in Minneapolis. The call was scheduled for 3:00 p.m., so I had to leave Stacey in the middle of a presentation about building a sales organization on steroids.

Jeff and I got on the phone and just started going bananas! Two guys crazy about real estate on the phone is combustible. Jeff has this energy about him that is contagious. You can't help getting fired up when talking to him.

During that phone call I shared personal stories. The strained marriage, the credit card debt, the Corvette, all the things I've written about to you in this book. Well, you got much, much more, but that's because Jeff and I only spoke for about forty-five minutes!

When we were talking right before the live Hangout, Jeff asked me if I'd be willing to share any of the stories I told him in our phone conversation. I said, "Absolutely!"

We went live and stuff just came pouring out, and then, in what seemed like five or ten minutes, our hour-long interview was over!

Within minutes I started receiving e-mails from agents telling me how good the interview was, how they have a similar story, how much they can relate, how inspirational I was.

I had several inquiries about coaching from people wanting to immediately hire me as their real estate coach. I was blown away.

There were so many requests for my Craigslist system, copies of my newsletter, the expired direct mail program, my 149-point prelist packet, our Good Life Tracker, etc.…so many that I built an automated delivery system to handle it for me!

Again, if you'd like any of the marketing materials mentioned in this book and in the paragraph above go to www.realestategoodlife.com. It's all there! No strings attached, no smoke and mirrors, no hocus pocus. All FREE!

The video is also on the website. I'd love for you to watch it and give me your feedback.

After the interview and the response from the real estate community, my self-esteem improved. It got me thinking that maybe it's time—time to write the book that's been in my head.

I've had the desire to write a book for many years. I've always come up with excuses as to why not to write it. They're really just diversions from the truth that has been deep down inside me.

I just didn't feel worthy enough to write a book. My limiting beliefs and the voice in my head always mocked me.

Now, here I am on the last stretch of completing this book and feeling great about it! Well sometimes…there's still that part of me that says people will hate it! At least now I've realized that the voice inside my head isn't actually me. It's my preprogrammed lizard brain.

The lizard brain is the oldest part of the brain and controls the limbic system. The limbic system controls our fight or flight mechanism. It's what kept us alive when our ancestors were being chased by dinosaurs!

The problem with the lizard brain is that it only knows how to keep you safe and out of harm's way. Writing a book, or being interviewed in front of your peers is viewed as a threat. The lizard wants to shut you down. His way of doing it is with self-doubt, worst-case scenarios, and simply just acting like a jerk.

There's another, albeit much smaller, part of the brain called the genius. OK, it's not actually called the genius, but that's what the Greeks called it back in the day.

The genius brain is where all the creativity comes from. It's where your true voice and self are housed. I like my genius brain! The bully lizard does whatever he can to keep the genius bottled up and at bay.

Now that I know these things, I have an advantage in pursuing my best life. An advantage in pursuing my happiest and most fulfilling life! This doesn't mean it's going to be easy. The lizard will never give up. There are ways to distract him and sometimes lull him to sleep, so the genius can come out and play!

There will be more on that in one of my upcoming books! Yeah—I said it! This is my very first book, and I'm already committing to many more!

Wow. Tangent. I'm sure you're used to it by now, right?

So I wanted to give a special thanks to Frank and Jeff. They don't know it yet, and they won't until they read this book…but they've helped inspire me to finally go for it!

Thank you guys!

CHAPTER 32

Eighteen Steps to an Extra $1 Million

The title makes an outrageous claim. But what if it were true?

If the following eighteen steps did produce an extra million dollars in commissions for you in the next five years or less, would you follow them? Would you implement them into your business?

The answer should be a resounding YES! Unfortunately, most agents, even when given a step-by-step process to follow, still will not follow it. Why? I wish I had the answer to that.

It reiterates what I tell my team over and over again: "There's a huge gap between what people CAN do and what people WILL do!"

So here's the eighteen steps to an extra million dollars. I look forward to your feedback.

1. Have and utilize a CRM system. CRM stands for Client Relationship Manager. There are literally hundreds of options out there for you, like Top Producer, Realty Juggler, Wise Agent, Contractually, etc. The key is to actually use it daily in your business.

2. Talk to fifteen people from your SOI each week.

3. Add two people to your database each week.

4. Write five handwritten notes each week.

5. Send out a printed monthly newsletter to your database.

6. Send one e-mail (video preferred) monthly to your database with a market update, short story, funny quip or insight, trivia contest, etc.

7. Send one e-mail monthly with a client testimonial/short story. Social proof and third party endorsements are as powerful a weapon as you can have in your arsenal.

8. Cards or calls. Send greeting cards or make phone calls to your database for New Year's, spring, the Fourth of July, Thanksgiving, and birthdays.

9. Complete the sixteen-page Real Estate Good Life Business Assessment Questionnaire.

10. Complete the thirteen-page Real Estate Good Life Goal Setting Extravaganza.

11. Sign and commit to the Declaration of Greatness.

12. Read four pages from a book every day. (This translates to six books a year.)

13. Journal five minutes a day two days a week.

14. Keep a peaceful mind ten minutes a day, five days a week. (I'd call it meditation but people picture tree huggers and yogis when you say that word.) Try it. Your life will change!

15. Practice gratitude Every Night ("I am grateful/thankful for…").

16. Practice good fortune every night. (Picture someone as you lie in bed each night and say to yourself, "I wish you good fortune" or "I wish you the best.")
17. Complete the Perfect Day worksheet.
18. Track three habits daily four days a week.

Imagine the difference you will make in your life and your business with these relatively simple steps.

I know what you're thinking, "Really Bart? That's it?"

Yes, that's it. Do what you're doing now and add the eighteen steps listed above. Chances are you're currently doing none of them consistently.

You remember the math we did back in Chapter 27 "Proper Communication." The simple act of adding two people to your database each week coupled with a specific plan of *proper communication* WILL change your life and business forever!

Now, please, I beg of you, go out and do it! Reading this book and painfully paging through all of my ridiculous childhood stories means nothing if you don't apply all the real estate stuff we just talked about.

The eighteen steps plus all the FREE stuff located at www.realestategoodlife.com is in your hands now!

You can access all the stuff listed above that you've never heard of, like:

- The Business Assessment Questionnaire
- The Goal Setting Extravaganza

- Declaration of Greatness
- Perfect Day worksheet

It can all be found on the website as well.

If you have any questions in general, or specifically about the eighteen steps, please e-mail me: bart@bartsellshouses.com.

Turn the page if you're ready for a little tough love...

CHAPTER 33

Tough Love

O K, one last closing thought on accountability, success, and what it takes to get it. Keep reading if you really want it. Keep reading if you are willing to face some of the harsh realities of building the Ultimate Lifestyle, and the difficult challenges and sacrifices required to get there.

If you cannot stomach the thought of hard work, turn the page and skip this musing. For those that understand that you have to be willing to live like most won't for the next few years in order to live like most others can't for the rest of your life…keep reading…keep listening.

What I'm about to say may offend some people (but not you), especially those of the "family comes first" ideology. So be it. It must be said. To reach a high level of success and riches in this business you are going to make tremendous sacrifices over the next few years, and you must employ accountability as your handler. You must submit yourself with total commitment.

As you build this business, everything in your life must be arranged to facilitate your ambition. You must have a commitment from your spouse, from your kids…a commitment that concedes understanding—understanding that you will get to work early and that you will be required to work late. With the vision of what is possible, you must practice delayed gratification. This means that you reap what you sow...but only after you've sown and sown and sown!

There is an ancient cliché: the hen contributes to breakfast, but the pig is committed to it!

You can earn a living selling real estate just by contributing, but you cannot reach the Good Life level without real commitment, both yours and the commitment of those around and closely tied to you, which is typically your family. They must buy in, support, and accept it.

Forget about living "in balance" for the next few years. You will be completely out of balance. Your business *will* get more attention than your spouse. Your business *will* get more attention than your kids. The out-of-balance part is not politically correct is it? They tell us we must live a balanced life. Take a close look, "They" are typically living a mediocre life. All you will have to do is live out of balance for the next couple of years.

Dedicate yourself to building a real estate business that will ultimately serve you, your family, and your lifestyle. Once it's built, you will then be able to live in balance for the rest of your life!

If you look closely you will find that there isn't a single person on or at the top of anything that didn't first live out of balance to get there. There's not a single one at the top of their profession, sport, or marketplace who lives a balanced life while in pursuit of the top of the mountain...in pursuit of the top of the pyramid. Not one. Ever. No CEO, no entrepreneur, no professional athlete, no rainmaking real estate agent. No one. If they claim they lived in balance while in pursuit...they're lying!

I've read hundreds of books over the past sixteen years, have studied about high-level success and top achievers past and present...in business, real estate, sports, and entertainment...from John D. Rockefeller to Andrew Carnegie, from Abraham Lincoln to Bill Clinton, from Michael Jordan to Wayne Gretzky, from Eminem to Lil Wayne. The message is clear and constant. They all possessed extreme commitment and accountability, and made sacrifices to achieve their greatness.

The trade-offs for success are tough. Few, and now fewer, are willing to make them, or even confront them. The same applies directly to the real estate sales business—thus producing a widening gap between the top, middle, and bottom of the real estate mountain...of the real estate pyramid.

Less agents are doing more business. Where you choose to be is up to you. Don't come here looking for the easy button, or the magic pill. I can't help anyone who won't be or isn't honest with themselves. Don't tell me how bad you want it unless you are willing to back it up with your actions! Live out of balance now, for the next few years...so you can afford to live in balance for the rest of your life. You will be able, accomplished, and deserving to live the Good Life.

Final Thoughts:

You now have in your possession everything necessary to build an incredibly profitable real estate business...and the thoughts and ideas and mindset to live a life that most only dream about.

A great craftsman never blames his tools. The tools are only effective if utilized. The tools are only effective if implemented. So now that leaves only you!

It's up to you. It's up to you to read, and reread, and most important-ly…to implement…to do something with what you have.

The difference between mediocre and meteoric is IMPLEMENTA-TION!

As Nike says, "Just Do It!"

This is the greatest small business opportunity in the world! Take advantage like I took advantage. I take advantage, I am taking advantage…every day! This business has provided me with an incredible lifestyle. But none of it would be possible without action, without risk, without dreaming.

I have created these things for myself. I don't rely on the government or the president or the economy.

No thanks, Mr. President…I don't need you to raise minimum wage for me to make a living!

No thanks, Mr. President…I don't need your food stamps or your free housing. I do fine for myself.

And oh yeah, Mr. President, if one day before I retire, the world's larg-est Ponzi scheme, Social Security, implodes…that's fine, I won't be needing that either!

What I've done did not require certificates, diplomas, college de-grees, or even permission slips from others. No, it wasn't and isn't easy or simple, but then I never expected it to be. I wouldn't want it to be! I like the view from the top, and it wouldn't be as nice if it were crowded.

Maybe luck was involved, if you consider the luck of being born on planet Earth, in the United States, and holding a license in the world's greatest small business opportunity…then maybe it was luck. Maybe there is a secret. Maybe there is one thing that if I shared it with you, your life would never be the same.

All right, it's true THERE IS A SECRET…

I already mentioned it earlier in the book. Maybe it seemed too simple to be considered a secret. But it is because most all agents, most all people, never figure it out.

The secret is: daily habits.

Anything you want to change or improve in your business, and more importantly in your life, can be achieved through daily habits. That's exactly why I included both daily habits and the perfect day in the eighteen steps.

Map your day out filled with concentrated bursts of productivity, coupled with the tracking of your daily habits and adherence to ideal habits… You Win.

Thank you very much for reading my very first book!

I promise you my commitment to continue to publish books and material specifically for the real estate agent. We are not only neglected by the public in general, but I feel we are neglected in the literary world as well.

From the bottom of my heart, I wish you the very best in everything that you do.

CHAPTER 34

Book List

The book is done! You've survived!

I truly do hope you've enjoyed the book.

Please feel free to text me with questions or feedback: 219-405-3768. Or e-mail me: bart@bartsellshouses.com.

If you have a second, I would be forever grateful if you gave me a glowing review (or your actual review, lol) on Amazon.

In parting I'd like to share with you some of my favorite books. You and I are both readers. I always like to hear about books that people like. Hopefully you'll enjoy my list.

Also, here's another recap of some of the FREE stuff you'll find at www.realestategoodlife.com.

Here's what you'll find when you register on the site:

- My Craigslist program that earned me an extra $98,000 last year.
- My Expired Listing direct mail campaign, a fifteen-step program that has delivered over six figures each of the past four years.
- Copies of my newsletter in PDF and Word format. The newsletter helped us go from 151 homes sold two years ago to 206 sold last year.
- The Good Life Tracker. The exact tracking sheet that my team uses to roadmap their daily activities.
- My 149-point prelist packet that has helped "presell" the team. We carry an average of 75–100 listings at a time.
- Declaration of Greatness. This document will blow you away, give you goose bumps, and send tingles up and down your spine. A MUST read!
- Free PDF copies of some of my favorite books.
- Ten-Minute Breakdowns. I read a lot of books. You may not have time to do so. I had one of my assistants sit for months transcribing my notes and highlights from a bunch of books. The breakdowns will deliver the heart of the message of each book to you while requiring less than ten minutes of reading each!

The website is going to ask you for your name and e-mail address. You will then be put in an automated funnel that will deliver the material to you. YOU WILL NOT BE SOLD ANYTHING!

Now, on to the book list. It's very difficult to create a list when you enjoy so many books. I gave it a shot, and this is what I've come up with:

Think and Grow Rich	—Napoleon Hill
Rich Dad Poor Dad	—Robert Kiyosaki
Total Money Makeover	—Dave Ramsey

Your Money or Your Life	—Joe Dominguez (1993 ed)
Start with Why	—Simon Sinek
The One Thing	—Gary Keller
Outliers	—Malcolm Gladwell
Tribe	—Seth Godin
Purple Cow	—Seth Godin
Blue Ocean Strategy	—W. Chan Kim
The Millionaire Next Door	—Thomas J. Stanley
The Richest Man in Babylon	—George Clason
How to Win Friends and Influence People	—Dale Carnegie
The 7 Habits of Highly Effective People	—Stephen Covey
The No BS Guide to Direct Marketing	—Dan Kennedy
The No BS Guide to Time Management	—Dan Kennedy
The No BS Guide to Wealth Attraction	—Dan Kennedy
The Ultimate Sales Letter	—Dan Kennedy
The Millionaire Real Estate Agent	—Gary Keller
E-Myth Revisited	—Michael Gerber
Walt Disney	—Neal Gabler
Einstein	—Walter Isaacson
Steve Jobs	—Walter Isaacson
Barbarians at the Gate	—Bryan Burrough
Den of Thieves	—James B. Stewart
Titan: The Life of John D Rockefeller	—Ron Chernow
The First Tycoon	—T. J. Stiles
The House of Morgan	—Ron Chernow
Andrew Carnegie	—David Nasaw
How to Get Everything You Want	—Jay Abraham
Man's Search for Meaning	—Viktor Frankl
The Power of Now	—Eckhart Tolle
The Catcher in the Rye	—J. D. Salinger

Yeah, I know, I probably left a bunch off the list that I'll remember later! All I know is that reading is one of the greatest pleasures one can enjoy. We only have an opportunity to learn from our own life once. With books we can learn from as many lives as we choose!

I wanted to also mention a few real estate–specific books for your reading pleasure as well:

Billion Dollar Agent Manifesto	—Steve Kantor
6 Steps to 7 Figures	—Pat Hiban
The 7 Levels of Communication	—Michael Mayer
Defeat Mega Agents	—Ryan Fletcher
Sell With Soul	—Jennifer Allan

Thank you!

THE END

Made in the USA
Lexington, KY
19 September 2016